Everyone wants to live a purpose-filled life, making an impact no matter how great or small. In *Who is That in the Mirror?* Darcey Kesner Hawkins takes you on a journey of transformation and rejecting labels, which will forever change your life if you let it. She shares how trauma led her to become a *Phoenix Rising*, and she empowers you through simple but important steps to overcome the imposter inside, discover who you truly are, and live authentically.

Kary Oberbrunner, author of Your Secret Name, The Deeper Path, Day Job to Dream Job, and Elixir Project

Growing up alongside Darcey Kesner Hawkins I thought I knew every facet of her life until I read her book "*Who Is That In The Mirror*?" Darcey takes us on her journey of self-discovery all the while giving the reader thought provoking questions. This is not a book that you will read just once. You will find yourself referring to it again and again.

Daelene Bunger

Darcey Kesner Hawkins has written a must-read book for anyone working on expanding their life. Darcey bravely leads us from tragedy to triumph and a clear plan to success.

Rev. Jackie Shein

"*Who is That in the Mirror?*", written by Darcey Kesner Hawkins, chronicles her journey of wearing labels or roles that society, and her family placed upon her to the extent she questioned what it meant anymore to be what Darcey refers to as her *authentic self.* In her book she delves into how she was able to break free from just living the expectancy of others that she allowed herself to exist and found fulfillment in achieving her own visions. I identified with her as for years I "allowed" my various roles as a grandmother raising my grandchild, as a supportive mother to my daughters, a good wife, daughter and sibling take precedence over things that I wanted to do for myself. I fell prey to the belief if I was the best at being there for others I would find my fulfillment in life. Why then did I feel such a huge void?

After being healed from an aggressive form of breast cancer that kept me confined to chemo treatments and regimens of just trying to survive, I realized I couldn't stay stagnant in my life any longer. I needed to find my passions and live a more intentional life as I witnessed Darcey doing. She inspired me by how she reached her own milestones in her life so much that I knew she was my *go to* for help. She guided me through several of her Intentional Living steps and helped me identify how to progress towards making my unfulfilled dreams a reality. Today, I have achieved two of my own milestones with the help of Darcey's strategic methods in defining one's authentic self. I look forward to continuing in my journey. This book is a must read!

Nani Ware - A more purposeful soul.

An honestly crafted personal guide for those seeking practical steps to become their authentic selves.

Michele Infusino

"*WHO IS THAT IN THE MIRROR?*" by author Darcey Kesner Hawkins, is uniquely more to me than you, but that said, so is she. Some will consider me biased, and it's with that awareness that I convey the depths of her passion and pain of peeling back the layers in finding her truest identity. I've been gifted the opportunity to see her a Phoenix Rising! Here she shares the many facets of her journey but unlike any book I've read, she pauses to help readers reflect on their journey and shares a system of success to assist others in finding their own. "WHO'S THAT IN THE MIRROR?" shines brightly as the gem that it is.

Mike David

Darcey Kesner Hawkins takes the reader on her personal journey of self-discovery in *Who Is That In The Mirror?* Hawkins shares the life, loves, and losses that challenged her throughout her life. She ultimately identifies the patterns that created so many roadblocks to her personal success and happiness. Darcey shares the tools she used and the path she followed to find the peace, fulfillment, and happiness we all seek. One does not need to have traveled the same road to benefit from her insightful and real-world solutions and apply her wisdom to our own lives. A compelling read, I highly recommend this book to all seeking greater understanding of how to be authentic, happy, and fulfilled.

Nansi Krauss, Editor

Darcey Kesner Hawkins is an amazing woman. She is candid and a loving spirit. This story is phenomenal. When you read this book, you will laugh and cry. She is a very caring woman, and she writes from her heart.

Donnette Martelle

WHO IS THAT IN THE MIRROR?

Overcome the Imposter Inside, Discover Who You Truly Are, and Implement Habits to Maintain Your Authentic Self

DARCEY KESNER HAWKINS

ILLUSTRATIONS BY

Wonda Ernsting

Printed in the United States of America

Published by Author Academy Elite
P.O. Box 43, Powell, OH 43035
www.AuthorAcademyElite.com

Softcover: 978-1-64085-544-1
Hardcover: 978-1-64085-545-8
Ebook: 978-1-64085-546-5

Library of Congress Control Number: 2019930353

Cover Artwork and Layout by Augusto Silva |
Photomanipulation by Rafael deBono

Illustrations by Wonda Ernsting

For my mother and father,
Margaret Kinoe Kesner and John Kenneth Kesner.

Without you I would never have been,
nor would I have become a Phoenix Rising.

I am blessed.

We have to confront ourselves.
Do we like what we see in the mirror?
And, according to our light,
according to our understanding,
according to our courage,
we will have to say yea or nay—
and rise!

Maya Angelou

TABLE OF CONTENTS

PART 4: OWN THE MIRROR!

APPENDICES

FOREWORD

Alfred Adler, (7 Feb. 1870 — 28 May 1937), was an Austrian medical doctor, psychotherapist, and founder of the school of Individual Psychology. Adler stated: "Every individual acts and suffers in accordance with his peculiar teleology ..." In other words, all behavior makes sense in the context of one's life and beliefs.

According to the National Children's Alliance, nearly 700,000 children are abused and neglected annually. This abuse and neglect impact on the lives of these children. And while the initial incidents are damaging, the most damage comes from what the child tells him/herself about the abuse. Such self-statements as "I am worthless" begin to form the basis of the child's core belief system. Adler called these beliefs "Mistaken Beliefs," and yet this core belief system becomes the basis on which the child filters information. Information that is consistent with the child's core belief(s) is kept and information that is inconsistent with core beliefs is discarded. Thus, layer by layer, the child begins to build a picture of him/herself based on the interaction of core beliefs and outside influences. This picture becomes the child's "public" persona. Beneath this public persona is the "mirror" image, the *Who is That in the Mirror?*

In her book, *Who is That in the Mirror?*, Darcey Kesner Hawkins takes readers on a journey of how the cultural and racial biases and trauma affected her. She then shares coping strategies to help others recognize and heal from their own abuse.

It takes courage to admit one has been abused and then to face the truth of one's past, including the willingness to uncover core beliefs and discard mistaken beliefs replacing them with the truth: "I am worthy", "I am valuable". Yet, it is a journey, that when undertaken, allows for deep healing and personal growth. We look at our pasts not to point fingers or to place blame, but to understand how I came to be where I am at this moment and who I am at this moment. We look at our pasts to discover our "Mistaken Beliefs" and to replace them with more valid, truthful beliefs. Thus, "I am worthless" becomes "I am worthy" and "I am valuable."

As Darcey's story unfolds, let it take you into your own heart and life and lead you towards healing.

Ann Van Dyke
Master of Arts in Psychology, retired psychotherapist, and author of "*Ride the Waves: A Caregiver's Journey*"

A NOTE TO THE READER

My name is Darcey. Thank you for spending your valuable time reading this book. I know everyone has a busy life filled with demands of work and family.

Your desire to read *Who is That in the Mirror?* will be time well spent. It has the potential to change your view of yourself if you let it.

The book is broken into parts. Parts 1, 2, and 3 are my memoir which contains the story behind the development of Part 4. Part 4 covers the Steps to Intentional Living which helped me find my identity, also known as my authentic self, and my purpose.

The most important point of Part 4 is the development of habits that work these Steps to maintain your identity and purpose. It's easy to forget you've lived as an imposter for a while and that you instinctively revert to old habits. As with most things, practice makes perfect. The Steps are designed to be repeated and some may be added to your Intentional Living Toolbelt.

An Intentional Living Toolbelt is a visualization of all the Steps; it's how you own your mirror. It will hold all your tools, skills, and techniques used in living an intentional life such as *Step 11 — Establish Your Intentions, Step 12 — Be Present,* and whichever ones will support your intentional living.

I use the word *imposter* to designate our identity as defined by society and family. It means we've not actively participated in deciding who we are in totality. For example, my father imprinted on me and my sisters the ultimate goal for a woman was to be a good wife and mother. This belief was reinforced by 1960's and 1970's society that surrounded my family. As you read through the book, you'll discover why he believed this was the truth.

It is important for you to know I use the metaphor of a mirror to universally apply to all things in your life that could reflect who you are. Clearly, a mirror will do this, but so does your behavior, what you create, your parenting style, your interactions with others, your interests and hobbies, your choice of profession, and especially your purpose.

The journey to discover who you truly are is not an easy one to undertake and complete. I lived as an imposter in my own life without realizing it because I experienced childhood and generational trauma in my formative years. Each day, each month, each year layered around my inner child so tightly my true identity was repressed.

Decades passed living as someone else until the growing unease was let loose with my mother's passing. I finally looked in the mirror, really looked, and didn't recognize the woman looking back at me. My countenance conflicted with my feelings of not being good enough along with the belief something was missing from my life. I looked successful, but I wasn't.

My journey of overcoming my imposter, discovering who I truly am, and establishing habits to maintain my authentic self was years in the making. Through divine guidance, I know my purpose is to help others find their true self and purpose by sharing my story.

This wasn't an easy decision to make as I share family secrets. I agonized over the telling. I put myself and my sisters through PTSD, and I know all who read this won't be supportive. However, if I help one person find their authentic self or realize their purpose, then I am successful.

But this depends on you.

If you're ready, let's start this journey together.

PART ONE

The Mirror

INTRODUCTION TO PART ONE

THE MIRROR

"You don't choose your family.
They are God's gift to you, as you are to them."

— Desmond Tutu

Our identity can be found by looking outward, but the best place to look is in the mirror.

Freedom! High school was over, and it was summer in San Diego. Warm beaches, salty air, and ocean waves were calling me. However, that was not to be my reality. My sister's friend was telephoning me about a clerical job downtown. I ignored the first interview, but her friend was insistent. This became my first job out of high school in a building with no windows.

I was a statistical typist in an accountancy firm. The women were the clerical staff and the men were the accountants. There was an older woman in the office who became my office mom. She took me under her wing and helped me navigate office politics.

Our friendship grew and she invited me to her house for parties. She talked of her grown children and what they planned to do with their lives. They weren't extensions of her and her husband; they had their own separate identities.

Was I supposed to have one, too?

This was an unsettling revelation at an early age but without the knowledge of where to look next, or even what to look for.

Part One — The Mirror is broken into three chapters. I share of how my family's generational traumas and societal expectations within two different cultures have been repeated for almost 100 years.

CHAPTER ONE

REMEMBER YOUR PAST

We receive traditions from our parents and extended families which are influenced by their trauma, cultural beliefs, and world events.

Do you have children? Are you determined not to repeat any experiences you had with your parents?

Do you remember your parents saying they wanted to raise you differently than their own upbringing?

(When I talk of not repeating experiences, I mean the average parental behavior; I don't mean neglect or abuse.)

I felt the same way. I said I would give my children all the experiences I never had. I said I wouldn't be so strict.

• • •

I forgot my parents were people with experiences before I was born. To be truthful, I never imagined them having a life before being my parent.

My earliest memory is my 5th birthday party. My family, except for my grandmother, and I were outside under blue skies on a sunny Southern California day. My dad walked with easy strides to the kitchen chair sitting in the driveway. He bent down, sunlight glinting off his black hair, and set my huge birthday cake on the chair waiting for this honor. It was a half sheet cake my mom baked for me. I vibrated with excitement because it was time to get my picture taken with my cake, our annual birthday tradition.

I don't remember who gave me the nickel, but this, too, was a yearly reward. The nickel was to celebrate my turning the big "5." Standing tall, I posed behind the chair with the nickel gripped in my sweaty little hand. As my mom, a petite Japanese beauty, positioned herself for the photo op, I felt the nickel slipping out of my hand. I squeezed my hand tighter, but when mom clicked the camera the nickel slipped out.

My stomach knotted as I watched my coin sink into the icing.

My gaze shifted up over what seemed like miles of slacks covered legs, over a buttoned-up shirt, over a smiling mouth into my daddy's twinkling eyes.

And suddenly everything was okay. My birthday didn't end. The cake was still edible. The party continued.

• • •

My dad was my hero. He was born in West Virginia in 1929 during the Silent Generation, a time when children were expected to be seen and not heard. Have you seen a child who is quiet all the time? Today, a quiet child means one who is doing something they shouldn't ... like writing their name on their bedroom wallpaper, but we won't name names here.

He was born into an old German lineage dating back to 1843 on his mother's side. His mama was born in 1911.

The social norms of the 1920's was a progressive time for women. They flirted more than their mothers and grandmothers ever did. Their body image went from being plump to prove their wealth and status to pencil thin, short hair, and caring for their skin in order to attract men. On the surface, things were changing, but views on premarital sex were not. Sex was allowed after one was married and then it was acceptable to have children.

My paternal grandmother, slender and fair skinned, didn't follow this edict. She was a rebel. She had a relationship with a man of questionable morals. He was a liquor runner during prohibition, and he didn't think twice about abandoning my grandmother before my dad was born.

Imagine living in an era with strict social rules and being "illegitimate". Neighbors likely used much more colorful and derogatory terms to describe my grandmother and my father. I can't fathom how it would feel to be known this way and to be ostracized.

Ninety years later *baby mama* and *baby daddy* are bandied around as if it were nothing. My heart breaks for my dad and my grandmother.

The societal hardship of his birth bonded my dad and grandmother closer together. He was a dutiful son, not because it was expected but because he loved her dearly.

My dad pushed past these invisible shackles and thrived. He didn't let being born out of wedlock restrict his goals. He was on the high school football team and while not a straight A student, graduated with the rest of his class.

During his teen years, dad almost lost his life in an auto collision He was hospitalized with a broken back and a metal plate was surgically implanted into his skull. He was literally hardheaded. Luckily, he healed well enough to enlist in the US Navy when he was 17 to fight in the Korean War. His first duty outside of taking care of his mom was being a patriot and defending the United States.

Other than the Enterprise, I'm not sure on which ships he served, but he was eventually stationed in Honolulu, HI, where he met my mom.

The cards stacked against him from birth did leave their mark on him, but he prevailed to be an honorable man with a wicked sense of humor.

My mom, a Japanese dark-haired beauty whose grace I wish I was blessed with, was born in Honolulu, HI in 1924. The Silent Generation really didn't apply to her as she was born in the Japanese-American-Hawaiian culture. This cultural heritage had its own social expectations of not only children but women as well. Both were considered subservient to the males in the household.

My mother's grandparents emigrated from Japan prior to 1918 with their three youngest children. Once they settled in Hawaii, they sent for my grandmother, called Oba-Chan in Japanese, who was 14 years old and their second eldest daughter. These two sisters traveled to Hawaii alone via ship.

They arrived safely and joined the rest of the family in a house on a hill above Pearl Harbor. My great-grandfather was a janitor at Tripler, the pink military hospital which seems to stand as a beacon on this part of Oahu, and my great-grandmother cleaned and ironed the uniforms of the military officers.

According to tradition, my Oba-Chan had an arranged marriage. When my mom was a toddler, my Oba-Chan divorced her husband for unknown reasons, and it shamed my great-grandparents. I don't have the details of what happened, but we do know when life presented problems, my Oba-Chan went to her parents for help. My sisters and I believe they would only help if she gave my mom to them to raise as their own daughter.

Mom believed she was the youngest of six children. She attended American school during the day, Monday through Friday, and Japanese school afterwards including Saturday. She always pressed this point with me when I complained about my homework. As mom reminisced, she shared of how much trouble she was in when she was caught not only wearing lipstick, but *red* lipstick. Being a rebel, or a teenager, she defied her father again by having her ears pierced. She didn't get away with this act of independence and was forced to let them heal.

One evening, my Oba-Chan, her three sisters, her brother, her parents, and my mom gathered as a family for dinner. No one knows what caused my great-uncle to be angry. He used his foul mood to change the course of my mother's life by blurting out:

"Tell her the truth; tell her, her big sister is her mother."

I can only imagine how mom received the news that shattered her life. At the tender age of 14, she was told by her irate "brother" that her oldest sister was really her mother. The people she considered to be her parents were her grandparents, and they had lied to her all her life. I'm not sure how much time passed before she realized she didn't know who her father was.

A short three years later, the Japanese bombed Pearl Harbor. Unlike the internment of many Japanese American citizens, our government foresaw the economic impact of interning the Japanese-American citizens from Hawaii and left them as they were, but restricted travel and imposed a strict curfew.

My Japanese family never felt comfortable in any situation they were in, whether it was riding the bus to work, attending school, buying groceries, or any of the other normal daily activities. They were regarded with suspicion, openly discriminated against, and lived their lives on alert. My mother never forgot how she felt being treated this way, and it forever shaped the choices she made.

• • •

I never thought about my parent's lives before I was born. Both my parents were only children, or as far as we know since they didn't know their fathers. There were no aunts, uncles, or cousins to fill us in on their childhood.

My parents' intentions to guide, raise, and love me, my two sisters, and my brother the best way they could was successful. Was it perfect? No. They internalized a lot of trauma and hurt they experienced. Some of the insecurities and pain peeked through. They were only human.

Their lives were filled with significant, life altering events. Both lacked the presence of biological fathers in their lives, both were labeled, and both were discriminated against. My dad almost died in an auto collision and survived a broken back. My mom had to deal with loved ones' deceit, unintentional abandonment by her mother, a strong patriarchal family life, and the day that "... will live in infamy."

All of this happened before they were 18 years old. Of course, this affected them and would affect their children one day.

The same could be said for my dad and mom's parents, my grandparents. The trauma they experienced shaped them as well. You can't blame them. They did the best they could with what they had.

Do you know your parent's story? Do you know what they've overcome to be who they are?

CHAPTER 2

REPLICATE THEIR ENVIRONMENT

With the greatest intentions, our parents wanted to create the perfect environment for us to be raised in. However, the beliefs and behaviors handed down to them are ingrained and cannot help but affect their parenting. Thus, they have replicated their environment to a degree.

Our parents do have a past. They have traditions they want to share with their children and grandchildren, but there are also actions they don't want replicated. Yet, life happens.

Imagine us floating over a small suburb. Shafts of sunlight spear through the trees from the lot across the street. Shrill voices cut the air drawing our attention, and we float closer making out the tops of two little heads sitting near a large military green electrical box. We draw closer still watching the heads grow bigger as their voices become clearer.

"Your sister is pregnant," The blond girl says.

"She is not!" The brunette girl says.

"My mom said she is! I bet you she is."

"I bet you five cents she's not!"

The scene before us fades to black. We float.

The dark film recedes from our vision, and we are now in a kitchen. We see flashes of avocado green appliances, a yellow wall telephone surrounded by flowery wallpaper, resin beads in orange, yellow, and green hang as a room divider, all lead us to a petite gray-haired woman sitting in an upright chair in the corner. She sits next to a rolling cart using it as a table for her belongings. She rises and shuffles out of the kitchen stopping by the small cabinet by the oven. She reaches into the now open cabinet pulling out a bottle of Boones Farm wine. She tucks it between her sweater and muumuu and continues shuffling out of the kitchen.

We float ahead of her and listen to her slippers slide on the plastic hallway runner. We're drawn to the buzz coming from the small room at the end of the hallway. The brunette girl is sitting on the floor in front of a TV which is playing white noise and wavy lines.

"I hear the music!" The brunette girl says as she looks starry-eyed at a teenage boy.

A pleased expression flits across the boy's face almost closing his almond-shaped eyes as he slips past the girl through the door. We watch his back as he moves down the hallway growing taller as he nears another room on the other side of the kitchen.

We float after him, hearing voices raise in anger as we near. We can't make out the words. A tiny black-haired woman is brandishing a broom at the now older teenage boy's head. The boy stumbles even though the woman never makes contact. The boy disappears.

We float back through the kitchen, around the refrigerator, and float through a closed door. We are in the garage. The little brunette girl is there with another girl a couple of years older than her. Their arms are crossed tightly around their middles as they look at a pair of yellow ten-speed bikes. Two men are in the garage.

"Girls, tell your grandpa thank you for the bikes." The slender dark-haired man says.

We look at the other, older man taking in his round belly and slightly off smile.

We look at the girls turning in unison staring at the older man with unsmiling faces.

• • •

As much as our parents don't want their own childhood visited upon their children, they can't help some of it leaking through.

My parents were ruled by the social mores of the mid-60s and early-70s in addition to the Silent Generation and mixed-cultural expectations of the Japanese in Hawaii.

For most of my childhood, I was happy and care-free. I lived with my mom and dad, two older sisters, Donnette and Daelene, my older brother, Michael, and my Oba-Chan in San Diego, California. The house with the most vivid memories was a single-family home across the street from my elementary school.

I was in my mid-twenties when it finally dawned on me we were a blended family. Donnette and Michael's father was of mixed heritage. Their Hawaiian blood showed more in Donnette's beautiful features while their Chinese blood showed more in Michael's. Their dad, who was Chinese, Hawaiian, and Irish, obviously wasn't my dad, but it didn't change my love for or the high regard I had for them. I never questioned the difference in our appearance; although, I'd love to have the more Hawaiian features Donnette has.

Being a blended family affected them. In the early 1960s emphasis was put on appearance, and their exotic backgrounds ensured they stood out in the mostly Caucasian area we lived in. The scrutiny they were subjected to made them self-conscious and shy. Did this lead to the choices they made? Or was being a teenager in that era the cause? I don't know.

My parents expected us to keep our personal business within the four walls of our house. This is when the secret keeping began.

Michael was heavily into drugs. Today, most of us can define an addict's behavior, and his behavior was typical. To help him and to calm our household my parents sent him to Teen Challenge in Hawaii. Was he hiding behind the drugs? Was he hiding at first, but then it gripped him and wouldn't let go? We will never know.

His drug use didn't matter to me; I idolized him from the time I could remember, and he loved me just as much. He was always ready to be my horse when I was a cowgirl. I was his audience when he turned his small black and white TV into a personal radio tuning in a local station. I was awed and amazed. Honestly, everything he did would have awed and amazed me. I was devastated to discover after he died he had shut me out of his life.

Donnette was pregnant without being married. She was 18 and it shouldn't have mattered. But in 1968, it was still a faux pas which my mom, especially, tried to deny. Mom swore me to secrecy with dire punishment if I told anyone. I was eight years old.

I know how I felt. I believed I was defending my sister's and family's honor by keeping our secret. Keeping quiet about my brother's drug use was universal knowledge in our family; no one had to tell me to keep it secret.

But how did they feel; particularly Donnette? She was shamed for her choice, and I know it affected her life choices from that moment. Today, it hurts my heart to think of the pain and anguish she and my brother went through. I wish so many things had been different.

My maternal grandmother, my Oba-Chan, lived with us as long as I can remember. I visited with her in her bedroom, and we'd play card games. The game of choice was Rummy where she always cheated so I could win. She taught me to play Paiute, a Hawaiian card game similar to poker, using a traditional deck of cards. We also played a Japanese card game called Hanafuda. The cards were a little smaller than a wallet-sized picture. The faces of the cards were colorful with flowers, kanji, and other symbols. The backs of the cards were black, and almost felt like mahjong tiles; they were smooth and had a little weight to them.

I flipped through her Japanese magazines while she prayed at her altar, she took me to Japanese movies (thank goodness there were subtitles), and I'd walk with her to a market a fair distance away.

She used a small corner section of the kitchen to sit in when she wasn't in her room. She had a rolling cart next to her chair which contained her kitchen belongings. She had a section of the fridge for her cold items; I loved her grape Hi-C juice. What I loved more was the sashimi (raw tuna) she purchased from the white truck that offered a wide variety of Japanese foods. It would stop at our house regularly. My best memory was sitting with her dipping our sashimi into a mixture of mayonnaise and shoyu—soy sauce to everyone else.

The *Japanese truck* drove by at a frequency I don't recall. It resembled a UPS truck, but it was white instead of brown. It became the *Japanese truck* because it was a grocery store on wheels with a selection of Japanese foodstuffs we couldn't buy at the local store. Oba-Chan treated us to rice candy, which I still buy for my six grandkids, and rock candy while she'd buy her grocery staples. She bought Japanese green tea, which was the most flavorful tea I've had, and different cuts of fish, which was where our sashimi came from. She also bought ingredients for sushi and other food gems.

My mother wasn't always kind to my Oba-Chan, her mother. Oba-chan's living conditions were evidence of it. Oba-Chan never came into the living room unless it was Christmas (but it could have been more since I was gone at least six hours a day at school), didn't eat dinner with us that I recall, and only had the corner of the kitchen to use. The only Japanese I heard spoken in the house was when they were yelling at each other.

Was this my mother's resentment rising to the surface from how she learned who her mother really was? Or was it because she didn't know who her father was? Or could it have been all the lies she lived with until she was 14? Or was it all of it combined? We'll never know as my mother passed away in 2008.

I never questioned my mom's treatment of Oba-Chan. I accepted this as the way they chose to live. I was always in her bedroom visiting with her when I wasn't playing Barbie's with my sister, Daelene, or outside catching tiny frogs that would end up in our washing machine because I forgot to dump them out of my pockets or reading books to win the summer reading contest at our local library or swimming at the pool in Chula Vista.

I felt my mother made a point of keeping our Japanese culture from us. She didn't make the effort to teach us to speak Japanese, we didn't celebrate Japanese holidays or customs, nor did she prepare Japanese food. Was this her way of distancing herself from the bombing in Pearl Harbor? Or distancing herself from the strict upbringing she experienced? Or could it be her way of combating the discrimination she suffered?

Oba-Chan, on the other hand, made Japanese food and shared some customs and beliefs with me. She tried to teach me how to make rolled sushi; my rolls looked like overstuffed seaweed worms spitting out white rice. She gave me the recipe for Umani, a Japanese vegetable and chicken dish considered to be good luck food. Today, we have this dish every New Year's Day.

The custom I follow every year is the one surrounding New Years. Oba-Chan's family would do all their cleaning and food preparation for New Year's Day the day and night before because the activities one chose to do on New Year's Day would be what you'll do for the year to follow. It was also important to eat good luck food on New Year's Day, so Umani became a fixed item on our menu.

I have more vivid memories with my Oba-Chan than I do with my dad and mom. Oba-Chan said she spent more time with me because my parents spent more time with Daelene. Right or wrong, Oba-Chan told me my parents weren't paying attention to me, so she was. I didn't notice their lack of attention because Oba-Chan kept me occupied.

But it must have affected me as the distance between my mom and I continued into adulthood. I loved her with all my heart, but we were never in sync as my Oba-Chan and I were.

What Oba-Chan didn't tell me was Daelene almost died at birth, and my parents were keeping a close eye on her. I understand this as an adult, but would I have understood it as a child? If Oba-Chan didn't spend time with me, would I have suffered from the lack of attention of a beloved adult? I don't know.

What I did suffer from was the sexual abuse from my step-grandfather when I was about ten.

I wasn't sure I would be able to share this fact with my loved ones which was a necessary step before I wrote about it. It took a long time to understand the importance of this heinous act against a child, me, and the pivotal role it played in my worldview.

This is another secret I've kept for decades. While my childhood was different than my parents, I was still living with the effects of trying to live within societal boundaries. Their environment was replicated to a degree no matter how they tried to keep it from us.

CHAPTER 3

CLEAN YOUR CANVAS

We all would like to believe when our child is born, they will have a life of opportunities, happiness, and dreams fulfilled before them. That it'll be up to the child to decide what they want to explore, achieve, or master with our guidance. We want to believe they're born with a blank canvas; they'll be their own person and design their own life purpose.

Most of us know our canvases are full of generational issues by the time we are born. Others of us, me included, aren't aware of it but know something is *off*. As we grow and develop, our positive and negative experiences grow with us.

My dad participated in one of my positive experiences. Exhilaration and a little bit of fear raced through my body as I rode my two-wheel bike down our street for the first time. My dad had his hand on the seat guiding me as my training wheels once had. After several minutes of this new freedom, I looked back to share my joy. My dad wasn't there. He knew I was ready to ride it alone, so he let me go. I wobbled at the realization, and bike and I hit the asphalt. So much was gained during this experience aside from the pain of kissing pavement; independence, self-confidence, and comfort knowing my dad would support me until I was ready to go it alone.

Yet, we all have experiences we don't share. The ones that cause damage to our body, mind, and spirit. One of my heaviest experiences is what my step-grandfather did to me. This experience overshadowed the positive ones and added strength to the negative ones. Eventually, I developed a negative worldview which colored how I saw myself and my life.

It was a secret. I wasn't supposed to tell. And I didn't. This is the little girl inside of me writing of my *secret*, cowering as the edges of the suffocating blanket hiding this atrocity is lifted. I made myself bury it, but it sat in the core of me leaking negativity.

The adult me is nauseous, disgusted, and wearing the face of anger at the thought of it all. How in the hell could a grown man lay hands on a ten-year-old girl?

No! Don't tell. No one is supposed to know.

In order to write the self-empowerment part of this book, I must navigate the misplaced guilt, self-disgust, and the myriad of other emotions roiling inside of me as I think of this trusted male who *touched* the daughter of his stepson. The stepson, my dad, who idolized this father figure from day one until my dad passed away. My dad honored him with the title of Father. This is the father figure that replaced the sperm donor. I don't know who is worse at this point, the absent sperm donor or the pedophile.

I wasn't allowed to tell. Even if I was allowed, I didn't have the courage to tell. How do you tell your parents of something you don't have the vocabulary for? I thought, somehow this is my fault.

I didn't believe this action could get worse, but I was wrong. I met with Daelene for lunch. I wanted to keep her aware of what secrets were to be revealed in my book. Acid burned in my stomach as I readied myself to meet her. Close to 50 years later and this horrific act still affected me.

Adults now, Daelene and I are close; we're almost the twins our mom dressed us to be.

Nervous, scared, and ashamed, I spit out in a short sentence, "Grandpa, touched me." My words still echoed in my ears as she didn't say anything.

I looked up into her emotionless face. My heart squeezed in my chest emitting real pain. She didn't believe me.

"I thought I was the only one." Her words floated lightly between us.

I was dumbstruck.

I couldn't breathe. I was sucker punched.

Sadness flooded my being for the loss of our innocence, and for keeping secrets far too long.

• • •

Afterwards, I pretended nothing happened. I buried it so I could be a normal child. But the horrific act nibbled away at the core of who I was for decades.

The pretense of normalcy flowed through our family. The dysfunction surfaced in bits and pieces so outwardly our life didn't change much. Donnette, my oldest sister, gave birth to her son. Dominic was the first baby in our home. I was fascinated by his tiny fingers and toes, his velvety soft skin, and the trust he had in me. I was an auntie at nine-years-old, and I was allowed to hold him. I thought this was the best thing ever until he started pooping. Most of my fascination ended with that bodily function.

Mom babysat Dominic while Donnette was working. As he grew older so did his mischievousness. Between our dog, Duchess, a black and white Boston Terrier, and my nephew, I couldn't hang onto my snack from my Girl Scout meetings. One of them would always steal it from me and I'd see the remnants either on the floor (dog) or around his mouth (nephew). One particular meeting we were given a huge chocolate chip cookie. I laid it on the chair by the front door so I could take off my sweater. When I turned around it was gone. I was literally foot stomping mad.

Michael came home from Teen Challenge. He was a healthy weight for being six feet tall, and he was clean and sober. I don't remember when he moved out. We lost touch during my teenage years as he was eight years older than me, and a lifetime older due to the drug use. He was living a life I couldn't imagine; fighting the pull of drugs every day.

Life was the same for my Oba-Chan; especially the undercurrents between her and my mother. My life was expanding outwards as I spent more time with friends than family. Reflecting, I wonder if I unconsciously designed it to be this way, or if it were a true adolescent coming of age rite.

Daelene and I became teenagers. She was in high school while I was in junior high as we're almost three years apart. One year she came up with the brilliant idea to share our school clothes money. I hope the sarcasm came through. It was brilliant for her. It was annoying for me.

We had a beautiful selection of clothes to wear. The perfect outfit I planned to wear always materialized on her body before I woke. The most annoying part? The clothes always looked better on her than they did on me.

My dad was the same stalwart provider and loving husband and father. He went to work early in the morning at National Steel Ship Building Company and was home every day by 4:30.

Dad enjoyed watching the news at the same time he was reading the newspaper. I saw him doing this daily, and I couldn't understand how he could do these two things at once. That is until my mom devised a new punishment for Daelene and me.

I don't remember why I was in trouble, but I do remember sitting on our uncomfortable, scratchy couch for hours. The same hours my dad watched all the versions of the news on TV, with a hot toddy on the end table next to his recliner. The news did not change, only the channel did and the newscasters. To this day I do not watch the news.

These and many more experiences layered over the abuse. Some experiences were happy and wonderful, and some were aggravating and maddening. The one thing they had in common was to help me bury and attempt to nullify the abuse.

An additional generational issue is the expectation of keeping family secrets. Of course, my family wasn't any different. However, my situation was different. I had my own secret I was keeping from my family.

I was adept at secret keeping. However, as I reflect on it almost 50 years later, it wasn't such a secret after all as it was expressed in my behavior.

I was an overachiever in junior high; I had to have straight A's. Some subjects, such as history and physical education, required extra effort, but the rest of the classes came easy to me.

An incident in 7th grade algebra may have been the catalyst of my self-injury journey. I had snapped my head to the right to look at a friend and excruciating pain ripped up my neck. The left side of my tongue went numb as an involuntary scream escaped me. The Algebra teacher walked up behind me and began massaging my neck in the middle of class, in front of my classmates. I froze in disbelief and went immediately back in time to the day another male authority figure touched me without permission.

My teacher's intention was to help. However, I cringed under his attention, as I did with my step-grandfather. The whole incident lasted a minute but felt as though time slowed and this unwanted attention would never end.

My friends talked about it all day, another thing that seemingly would never end. I turned red and that kept the conversation going. No one knew what the cause of my blood infused face was.

As with the flow of acrylic paint on a canvas, so it is with life's experiences. Sometimes, there's exactly enough water mixed in the paint so the brush glides over the canvas. These are the enjoyable, happy experiences. Other times, the brush and paint drag. These are the trauma laden experiences. All experiences lay over one another covering up what's underneath, but the impact always bleeds through.

This is the point in my life when my experiences were gliding. I was in 8th grade and enjoying more opportunities to exist outside of my family. I was more comfortable in my skin and enjoyed talking to boys. What 13-year-old girl doesn't?

I was part of a close-knit group of kids, some were old friends from when I was as young as nine, and some were new friends from other elementary schools. We formed a warm bond partly out of necessity, and because most of us were military brats. Some of us had classes together, but we all hung out together at lunch. We all had a fluid friendship with a lot of joking, laughing and talking.

One of these new friends, Joe, was a boy with sandy colored hair, tan skin, and glowing light blue eyes. My heart sped up when Joe spoke; his slight southern drawl was a novelty that drew me in.

Our adolescent world was expanding beyond home and school. We went roller skating at Rocket Roller Rink on Friday nights, along with going to the movies. Joe and I gravitated to each other during these outings. Soon we were dating.

One of the best memories I have is sitting with Joe in the packed theater on Palm Avenue watching the premiere of Jaws. There wasn't an empty seat in the house. Joe was sitting at the end of our row, I was next to him, and a man was sitting next to me. Tension increased as the music builds when Brody, Chief of Police on Amity Island, examines a listing boat. Leaning forward, I gripped the armrests. A decapitated head pops out. Screaming, I jumped throwing my arms out, grabbing both Joe and the stranger next to me. Both screamed and jumped, and I watched as the screaming and jumping *waved* throughout the theater. I still get a chuckle at this memory.

With the additional freedom from my parents came more expectations, and they were strict. If I was home one minute late, they put me on restriction for 30 days. I believed this was their attempt to control me and prevent me from making poor choices regarding drugs, sex, and alcohol.

I was programmed to take authority figures seriously. When they said I was on restriction for 30 days, I sat on restriction for 30 days. It never occurred to me to sneak out. I would stick my head inside a novel, and I was transported to another world. What adventurous spirit I had was constricted with my inner child.

My own self-limiting beliefs restrained my inner child, also. I kept comparing myself to my sister, Daelene, and found myself lacking. Daelene was popular, beautiful, and outgoing. I disliked her; I realize now it was because she was everything I wasn't.

The stress to achieve perfection in the different parts of my life was wearing me down although I didn't know it at the time. The drive to be perfect came from me, and me alone. I'm not sure of its origins or why it afflicted me, but it wore me down to the point of several suicide attempts, and no one knew. Another secret I couldn't and wouldn't share with anyone.

The trauma of the abuse didn't lessen. Instead, my world grew bigger around it. I liken this process to how an onion grows. The center or core of the onion is the trauma which I experienced as a ten-year-old. Layers of *flesh* grew around it as I aged. The quality of the *flesh* wasn't healthy as it was comprised of the dysfunction within my family, the need to keep secrets, and the inability to know who I truly was.

By the time I was in high school the trauma was firmly cocooned within me, buried within layers of everyday experiences. Between my parent's need to control me, my fear of not being in control of my life, and other behaviors I was a mess.

The knowledge that I had the power to clean all of this off my canvas never penetrated my 15-year-old worldview.

PART TWO

The Person in the Mirror

INTRODUCTION TO PART TWO

THE PERSON IN THE MIRROR

"When I let go of what I am, I become what I might be."

-Lao Tzu

In the latter part of our teen years, we're expected to build a solid framework of who we are.

Yet when we look at ourselves in the mirror what we're really seeing is the framework of our parents, the environment that we grew up in, and the familial connections.

As we embark on our adult journey, we should be clarifying who we are. This is normally done through testing the waters of the choices before us, i.e. choosing between vocational or traditional college, spending more time with our friends than our family, entering the workforce or the military, or a combination of several things.

As we mature, we should have input from a trusted adult(s) to help guide us and to provide us with objective feedback. In a perfect world our parents, grandparents, or school counselors would fulfill this role. They would offer guidance to help keep us grounded, help us build and materialize our dreams, and help us to be accepting of deviations to our path.

Our experiences from our first step onto the road of adulthood should start molding us into the adults we will become. However, childhood trauma leaves an indelible mark upon us. It's up to us to recognize it, accept it, and respond for our best and highest good.

In the next three chapters, you'll journey with me as I make the transition from teenager to young adult, from being powerless to empowered.

CHAPTER 4

ACCEPTING THEIR IDENTITY

We are not the creators of our identity. As we gaze into our mirrors, we believe in the image reflected back. We don't question where it came from not realizing it was molded by our family, our environment, and our experiences.

I was sitting in my Oba-chan's bedroom one day. I don't remember what day it was or how significant it would be. She was pale, her face blended into her gray poufy hair. She was a little fatigued, achy, and had sharp pain in one of her fingers. As always, she was wearing one of her muumuu's, a sweater and her tabi's (Japanese big toe socks).

I sat next to her on her single bed. She placed her smooth, tiny hand in mine after I asked to see her finger. The skin was stretched taut on her right ring finger. A little beyond the base of her nailbed was a blister that laid flat against her skin. With the lightest of touches,

I stroked the spot to see if it was raised. Oba-chan sucked her breath in from the pain. I knew something was really wrong, but I didn't know how to articulate it. All I could manage was, "You need to go to the doctor."

I don't remember how long it took for her to see her doctor, or how long it took for them to diagnose her. I do remember the horrible diagnosis. She had lymph node cancer. In 1977, cancer was a death sentence. Something else I knew and remembered.

When I wasn't in school or at my after school job, I was with Oba-chan. I had stopped participating in the high school drill team in my junior year, so I didn't have any extracurricular conflicts. Not that it would have mattered as I wouldn't have chosen it over my her, my second mom.

One evening we sat on her bed staring at the wall. The playing cards didn't come out. She wasn't praying at her altar. She looked over at me, tears spilling over her cheeks.

She spoke without a trace of a Japanese accent, her words clear, and pain filled.

"Darcey, I don't want to die."

She didn't see my tears as she buried her face in her hands. Instinctively, I reached out and hugged her to my chest. Her frame was light, small, and fragile. I squeezed her as tightly as I dared.

"I'm sorry. I'm sorry." The words fell quietly, mantra-like from my lips.

Later that night, I went to my mom for help.

"Mom, Oba-chan said she didn't want to die. What do I do?"

"Stop spending so much time with her. You're reminding her she's going to die." Was my mom's answer to the pain and helplessness I felt.

I was crushed. It was me. It was my fault. I was reminding Oba-chan she was dying, but I craved spending time with her. Losing her was losing my mother, and I needed the warmth of her presence, to hold her when she cried. I realize now I was being comforted as much as I was comforting.

I was upset my mother would stop me from spending time with her, but at 17 I thought my mother knew best. I abandoned my Oba-chan.

As I reflect on it as an adult, I see the pain my mother was going through knowing she was watching her own mother dying. Her words and tone were grief-laden. She didn't intend to hurt me but wanted to give whatever peace she could to her mother, my Oba-chan.

There was a sterile smell in the room. Fluorescent ceiling lights illuminated the corners. The hospital bed dominated the space, and Oba-chan's tiny body only covered a fraction of the mattress. Standing at the side of the bed, I saw Oba-chan's blood had backed up into the IV needle and tubing; her hand was swelling. I was angry. The nurse needed to come in.

"They have to come in now." I demanded. "Her blood is being sucked up into the IV."

"Darcey, lower your voice." My mother said.

"Mom,..." I began.

"Stop it. You're making a scene." She was angry, too, but at me. My father stood silently by.

I stormed out of the room. I knew Oba-chan was going to die. My chest tightened, my heart raced, and I wanted to run away. I began pacing the hallway. I moved fast and was at the end of the hallway before I was ready to be there. I spun on my heels and headed back to her room. On this pass, I noticed the pay phone which had been mounted there the whole time.

I needed to call my sisters, Daelene and Donnette. I don't remember our conversation. I do remember the misery in my heart and the desperation in my words to get them to the hospital to say goodbye. Neither one could make it. They were both mothers and couldn't get away.

The next morning, Sunday, January 29th, 1978, at 4:10 a.m. my Oba-chan passed away. I lost her when I was 17 years old and a senior in high school. She was the loving mother figure in my life, and I was overwhelmed. I lost one of my champions on that January day.

Nights dragged after my Oba-chan passed. When I shut my eyes, I would see us playing Rummy, walking to Brown's Market where she bought me whatever I wanted on her limited budget, and me sitting on her bed as she prayed to her ancestors. It took me hours to fall asleep. In contrast, my days were crammed with graduation activities, finishing up classes, and spending time with Joe, again. I was tired by the end of the day, but sleep was still elusive.

I blamed myself for her death. I know it's irrational to believe I was the cause of her death, but I kept replaying my choice in my mind. If I hadn't pushed her to go to the doctor, she would have lived. In some respects, I was mature for my age, and in others, I was still thinking as a child.

This is the center of my dysfunction—chronologically growing older but rooted strongly in the past. I was that 10-year-old girl still believing I could have stopped the unstoppable. It was my fault for allowing it to happen. I had the control, therefore, I deserved what happened to me. This disparate thinking would govern my choices for decades.

Joe and I had transitioned from junior high to high school as sweethearts. He became the focus of my days, and I loved it. I had healthy attention focused on me, and I was able to give it back. I was always with him and less and less with my girlfriends.

Eventually, new friends didn't think of me without thinking of Joe. I was an extension of him—I didn't have an identity separate from Joe. I was literally known as *Joe's girlfriend* in high school except in my homeroom and on drill team. I didn't have close friends, and more importantly close girlfriends I could open my heart to. I was isolated but didn't realize it until many years later when a friend shared her perspective of our high school years. I had chosen this life, and it was another fear-based decision.

Over the years I gradually adopted Dad's worldview of finding a job, the perfect man for me, and ultimately getting married. Attending college was never one of the choices. Remember, his worldview was shaped by his family dynamics. His father abandoned not only him but had abandoned his mother as well. Dad wanted us to be taken care of—this was his ultimate goal. Joe believed something similar so our dreams coalesced around marriage and children.

I didn't realize I wasn't thinking for myself. I didn't realize I was latching onto what I perceived as a lifeline.

Before we graduated, Joe agreed to an early enlistment in the Air Force. He was making plans for our future. My future planning consisted of waiting for him to have everything in place for us to be married.

At some point during high school, we developed an understanding that we'd get married after graduation.

Right after high school, Joe went to boot camp in Texas, and then to technical school in Colorado. After graduation, I worked as a statistical typist in an accountancy firm. I almost missed this opportunity as I ignored the first interview. I was intimidated by the one-way streets I'd have to travel to find the business office. This was pre-MapQuest days let alone GPS. It was *pull out the map you bought at the gas station* days. The one-way streets were like tunnels with no way to escape. And I did turn the wrong way, but luckily it was after the interview. I was stuck facing oncoming traffic in a narrow street, with cars parked along the curbs and having nowhere to turn. It was amazing what my gutless Subaru could do when I whipped the steering wheel over and over in a miniscule section of downtown San Diego.

Joe's first duty station was Kadena AB, Okinawa, Japan. He worked diligently through the paperwork mire for permission for me to join him. I filled those eight months with working, watching TV, and sleeping my life away. Joe was gone, and I was adrift. I didn't have the bonds of friendship with any of the girls I went to high school with; it was my fault for not reaching out to them. I was lonely and was in bed after dinner at 5:30 pm. I didn't see this behavior for what it was—depression.

My feet and ankles wobbled slightly as I stood to gather my belongings. I had been traveling for 24+ hours flying from Los Angeles, through Hawaii and Guam and into Naha Airport, Okinawa. My apricot colored skirt, blouse, and white slide heels weren't the attire of a seasoned traveler, but I looked cute—when

I boarded the plane. Now I was travel worn, my hair mussed, my makeup smeared, and my outfit crumpled. Clutching my carry-on, I inched down the aisle with the other passengers, mostly Okinawans, toward the door. I squeezed in behind the large man who had commandeered five of the six seats in our row as a bed.

I disembarked and spotted Joe. All the distress I experienced melted away in his embrace, but I didn't know the root of my insecurity was still festering within me.

Okinawa was a tropical paradise to me—an 18-year-old girl whose first solo trip away from home covered over 6,500 miles to an international destination. Was my perspective skewed? Possibly. I only knew what I saw. The Pacific Ocean was still within reach. Granted, the opposite side of it. The baby blue sky competed with the varying hues of teal and sapphire in the ocean, and evergreens populated the pockets of forests surrounding our apartment at the end of Kadena Air Base's runway.

Months went by as we tried to meet the administrative demands of the American Consulate. Our birth certificates weren't official, yet I only knew of the one which carried the imprint of my baby feet, and Joe was in the same situation. Writing to the various agencies housing our official birth certificates took time. As did their processing of our requests. Late winter turned into late spring before we received what we needed.

Meanwhile, Joe worked, and we played on the white beaches, in the warm surf, and under the hot tropical sun. I should have been content, but a small discomfort kept me company for the nine months I lived on Okinawa. I was not doing my part to support our relationship; I wasn't working. My sense of self-worth diminished, and my identity was still buried. I believed these things even though I knew I couldn't work under the provisions of Joe's tour of duty in Okinawa.

Finally, we had all our proper documents. We went to the American Consulate and completed more paperwork, we were then directed to City Hall in Naha—the capital of Okinawa—for more of the same, we went upstairs to visit with Okinawan nationals who turned out to be our witnesses (witnesses of what I wasn't sure), and through gestures we were told to go back downstairs to City Hall where we were pronounced married.

The whirlwind of activity was over, and we found ourselves on the front steps of City Hall. In jeans and t-shirts instead of my white dress, we exchanged rings and kissed. I was joyous our bureaucratic journey was over except for one last step. Time to go back to the American Consulate to have my passport stamped. I was officially *Mrs. Joe.* That name and singular identity followed me through most of our marriage. I was an extension of my husband; not an individual person.

Our next duty station was in England. We went from an island, Okinawa, where most of the people looked like my relatives, was ruled by an Emperor/Prime Minister, was tropical, and similar to San Diego to an island whose weather dropped lower than I had experienced, was ruled by a Queen/Prime Minister, and whose historic buildings dated back before the United States was founded. I had entered the doorway to another culture.

The Bed and Breakfast (B&B) we moved into was an elderly couple's two-story home. They made a point of opening their home up to incoming and outgoing American military couples. Their walls were covered in wallpaper with tiny flowers. I admired a painting of a horse in the dining room when I went into breakfast the next morning.

"That's a gee-gee." Ms. Catherine, the Inn Keeper, told me. She continued to share the English words for commonplace things like *boot* for car trunk, and *windscreen* for windshield.

Homemade marmalade was on the table with other fruit preserves for our toast. The sweetness and tartness lingered on my tongue. I added scrambled eggs and sausage to my plate. So continued our days there until we found permanent housing. Well, permanent until it was time for us to move to our next duty station.

We found housing on Glover's Lane, so we had to say goodbye to our Inn Keepers. Unique to this area, and possibly to England as a whole, the English people named their streets after the work done there. We lived in an area where gloves had been made.

Joe reported for duty to his new squadron right after we settled into the B&B. He was charismatic so made friends quickly. Soon, we were invited to BBQ's and parties, but socializing was difficult as I wasn't comfortable with who I was. I still felt *less than* as I compared myself to them, especially the female military members. I sat on the outskirts of the group only answering when spoken to. In hindsight, they had to believe I was a snob. I soon was known as *Mrs. Joe*, but this time it was my fault as I didn't reach out to become friends with anyone.

At this duty location, I was acknowledged as a dependent so I could work. I went on the hunt for a job, but there was none to be had. To keep busy and keep my skills current I volunteered for the Red Cross. The Red Cross placed me in the military personnel office supporting whoever needed it, but volunteering wasn't enough to drown out the nagging feeling I wasn't enough. I needed a paying job to validate my contribution to my marriage and to myself.

The Air Force was the only employment available. I thought "why not enlist?" and bring value to my marriage. My recruiter told me I had tested well and was best suited as a computer operator. But when he put the contract in front of me to sign my heart started racing. I was signing my life away for four years. I breathed in short gasps and felt queasy. I had an anxiety attack. I don't know why it bothered me so much to know I couldn't walk away from a job for four years.

My first duty station after boot camp and tech school was back at RAF Bentwaters with Joe. We were fortunate I was stationed with him. While the Air Force tried their best to reunite spouses, there were no guarantees.

Within months of my return, we became pregnant. Having a child with both of us active duty posed issues we hadn't thought about before. With these issues in mind and other things that happened while I was active duty, I chose to separate from the Air Force before I gave birth.

Was this how my path was supposed to be? A paying job wasn't in my future yet. If I had been more mindful, I could have been open to the messages from Creator.

I embraced motherhood with every essence of me. I began living for this boy, my son, Joe Jr. I had my purpose. I was a mommy and that's all that mattered.

Did I solve my issue? No, I buried it back into the fleshy outer folds protecting my core once again. I was content to keep it this way for decades.

CHAPTER 5

REFRAME YOUR REFLECTION

We have the power to live our purpose. Own your path-reframe your reflection.

How many of you are parents, employees, bosses, students, or other labels you identify with? Do you ever question if you're living in cognizance with your true self and purpose? Each choice you make without knowing and believing in yourself is a label you wear. I don't mean to imply, especially being a parent, you don't give 100% to this part of you. However, until your purpose resonates within your heart, you're not giving the very best of yourself to this facet of you.

When your purpose resonates it means there is no doubt or fear you're living true to yourself. It means when your human existence is over you have no regrets, no 'I wish I had pursued a gift God has given me.'

One of the first labels we may wear as an adult is *spouse* and *parent*. I did and absorbed them.

Sitting in my living room chair on the afternoon of March 24th, 1982, I felt the first twinges of pain across my belly. Even though I was three weeks overdue, I didn't think this was the onset of labor. The pain wasn't intense, so I thought it was a muscle spasm. Joe walked in the house after work and we ate a dinner I don't recall making. At the end of the evening, I waddled upstairs to bed, Joe came to bed later. The twinges were steady, slowly increasing in intensity, but they were easily managed, and I fell asleep.

The next morning the pain was tolerable, and I told Joe to go to work. This was a mistake.

We didn't have a house phone and while cell phones had been invented, we didn't have over $3,000 to buy one. Joe would be gone for 10 hours that day. What was bearable pain at 5 a.m. was excruciating by 5 p.m. and the contractions were about five minutes apart.

I met Joe at the door when he returned home that evening. One look at me and he bundled me into our little red car. There was no time to go to the military hospital at RAF Lakenheath—it was over 40 miles away. Off we went to a local English hospital.

A medical staff member ushered us into an examining room and left. Minutes later a doctor walked in. He checked me and said "You're only 6 cm dilated. Go home and come back later." I looked at him in disbelief—he was sending me home. "Someone will come in with discharge papers." he said. He was out the door as quickly as he had come in.

Joe and I exchanged glances. I put on my coat and slid off the exam table. We waited about 10 pain filled minutes for the discharge papers. Finally, the door opened once again, and another doctor came in.

"Please, get on the table. I want to check you before you leave."

I climbed ungracefully atop the table. He checked me, and I heard the shock in his voice, "You're 8 cm dilated. Sisters, admit her."

I was whisked away into unknown territory, in powerful rolling pain with small increments of relief. I didn't know where Joe was. Sisters, the English nurses in white uniforms, blue belts, and blue caps, helped me undress and put on a hospital gown. I was alone and there was nothing familiar to me. My heart sped up. The nurses settled me in a warm hospital bed in my own room as Joe burst through the door. I began to calm.

Two Sisters darted towards him saying he'd be better off in the waiting room with a cup of tea while shooing him out the door. I was climbing out of the labor bed to stop them. Joe wasn't going anywhere. I didn't make this baby alone, and I wasn't going to deliver him alone. They realized the crazy American girl was serious when she said he wasn't leaving.

Since my water didn't break on its own, a Sister used a tool to break it. Water barely leaked out, and the Sisters exchanged a look full of import which I didn't understand. They both spoke at once assuring me everything was going to be ok. Of course, I became more anxious.

At some point before midnight, I dilated to 10 cm and was declared ready to give birth. They wheeled me into the delivery room. The table was a cold, stainless steel slab very reminiscent of an autopsy table. The stethoscope the doctor used had a plastic cone at the end of it. It seemed they only used it when I was in the middle of a contraction. A prism-shaped plywood back support was all they had as the table did not articulate. It reminded me of the Swiss candy bar, Toblerone.

I don't know how long I was in the delivery room. Someone kept telling me to push—I wanted to scream at them I was pushing, that I couldn't push any harder. I was tired, and pain was painted in every fiber of my being. Poor Joe stood and rubbed my low back for hours. Later I was told that back labor is the most difficult. At that moment it didn't matter to me—pain was pain and it was eclipsing everything. Someone gave me gas for the pain—I latched onto it like a leach—six hours of hard back labor was more than I could deal with.

I was using too much of it. Someone took the gas away from me because it was impeding the delivery. Whispery words floated in the air—*we'll use forceps.*

Forceps? The word registered through the mist floating in my brain. Images of babies' indented heads wafted through my mind. No one would use forceps on my baby. I bared down and pushed with all my strength.

"Stop. Stop pushing." What? Now I was to stop pushing? I couldn't get the fog lifted from my mind. None of this made sense.

"You're going to tear." I didn't understand.

Then it all clicked into place as the doctor performed a medical procedure to stop me from tearing.

Our son, Joe, III, was born at 11:45 pm on March 25th. He was 10 pounds 11 ounces, and 19 inches long. His head was 38 cm around. This boy could have pulled on a pair of cowboy boots and walked out of the delivery room.

Nine months later we were back at the same English hospital, but our needs were different. Baby Joe had been an active baby and had attempted his first steps. Now he was listless, ran a fever with tears oozing from his eyes—he had never cried like this before. Baby Joe was very sick, and both Joe and I were frightened.

The staff in the emergency department zipped him away with Joe and me trailing behind. Once we reached a room, they laid him in a crib, safety pinned his tiny arm and IV to the sheets and left him in his diaper. I sat next to his crib and reached in to touch him. My hand was two inches from his little body, and I could feel the heat radiating up. My fear increased.

A Sister rolled his crib out of his room and said they would run tests. Time slowed, and we waited. Baby Joe was brought back to us after a bit, but it had felt like eons. The Sister said they'd have results soon.

I don't remember if it was the Band-Aid on Baby Joe's low back or if the Sister told us, but we knew they had performed a spinal tap on our baby without our permission, hell, without even telling us.

This is when I learned about one aspect of socialized medicine. The doctors don't ask the parents' permission to perform any medical procedures. Joe and I were scared and angry. Joe notified his squadron, and it was elevated to the military hospital commander. I know the commander spoke to the people in charge at the hospital, but I don't know what the outcome was.

The doctor finally came into Baby Joe's room and shared the awful news—Baby Joe had strep pneumonia and septicemia (a serious bloodstream infection). We had almost lost him. Yes, their methods were unorthodox to us, but they saved our baby's life. And, I will be forever grateful.

It was shortly after this, we received orders to Reese AFB, Lubbock, Texas. The Air Force packed up our household goods, we cleared the base and began our journey to our new duty location with a new member in our family, our baby boy. We detoured to San Diego to introduce Joe Jr. to the rest of his family.

While we were visiting in San Diego, we bought a compact car with a stick shift—any other details about the car is lost to me other than it was tan in color. Joe thought it'd be a great idea to teach me how to drive it on our way to Texas. I was up for the challenge.

We made good time with Joe driving and stopped at a McDonald's for lunch. Baby Joe, who was almost one liked the idea, too. It was my turn to drive after we finished lunch. I was pretty good on a flat stretch of road—I didn't need to have the balancing act between the left and right feet over the clutch and accelerator.

As with most parking lots, this one was flat. The difference was in its exit. It had an upward incline and once cleared of it we would enter the two-lane highway.

A high school memory flashed in my mind. I was driving Joe's Chevy Nova to his football game one afternoon. His Nova had three gears on the column versus the stick shift on the floor something I had never experienced before. I was doing great until traffic slowed on the highway. I slowed, too, downshifting with ease. However, that balancing act between the feet was nonexistent. I stalled the Chevy on the highway. My head whipped up to look in the rear-view mirror and we were lucky, none of the cars behind us were close. I tried a couple of times to get the damn car to go and was close to panicking. Finally, my feet cooperated and with a screech and a smell of rubber we were in forward motion again, barely ahead of the closing traffic.

With that memory in my mind, blood rushed into my face and my heart began to beat faster. I could do this. I balanced the clutch with my left foot and the accelerator with my right. A semi-truck was coming—I had plenty of time to get onto the road. We lurched up the incline and the car stalled. The semi was still coming. After starting the car, I gave it more gas than it needed, and we jumped onto the highway right in front of the semi.

I almost wiped out our little family of three in our little stick shift car from San Diego.

Joe was white-faced, Baby Joe didn't have a care in the world, and I continued to grip the steering wheel like grim death driving us to Lubbock.

We arrived safely in Lubbock, home to Reese AFB, and moved into our two-bedroom apartment. Joe in-processed to his new squadron, and I settled us into our new home.

It was time to find a job with set hours so I could be home to take care of Little Joe and be the epitome of a house-wife.

With a little research, I found my answer. A federal job would allow me to follow Joe more effectively and give me the stability to take care of our little guy. This process was easier said than done. A kind clerk at the personnel office walked me through the lengthy steps to get my name on one of the Office of Personnel Management's (OPM) clerical registers. The first step was to take their test. This is when I found I was pregnant with our second child.

Weeks passed before I was armed with my score and application. I applied for all the open positions.

My name was added to hiring certificates, I was interviewed, and I was non-selected each time. My confidence dwindled with each non-selection. What was wrong with me? I was a strong typist—78 wpm. Yes, I was young, but I was adaptable, and it was easy for me to learn. This wasn't rocket science, for Pete's sake. Why didn't anyone select me I pondered as I peered down at my growing belly.

I was close to delivery, and I gave up looking for employment until after our daughter was born.

Weeks passed and my due date of March 1st came closer and was gone. I poured my frustration out to my OB exactly on the seventh day post my due date; I couldn't wait three weeks for our daughter to be born. My doctor explained she would strip my membranes, a medical procedure to start labor. Joe and I looked at each other—we hadn't brought my overnight bag. Joe left instantly.

Labor was immediate and painful. The contractions were getting closer and closer together. This was pre-epidural days—I felt each contraction. I looked up and saw the mobile they had installed to keep birthing mothers occupied. I focused on it to the exclusion of everything else. I was meditating on it so completely the contractions slowed. My doctor yelled at me to stop—to allow labor to continue.

Joe almost missed the birth of our baby girl when he went back for my bag. From start to finish labor and delivery was under three hours for our daughter, Victoria, compared to the 28 hours for her brother. Victoria, all nine pounds and seven ounces of her, burst into this world. When all became quiet after her birth, my OB came to me and said, 'there's a good chance your next baby will be 12 pounds'. This was the end of my child bearing years—giving birth to a 12 pound child was definitely not in my future.

Isn't it ironic the first interview I went on after I gave birth was the first job I was offered? I started my civil service career as a Clerk-Typist in the 64th Student Squadron supporting all the undergraduate pilots in their training. This could have been by design as they were a great bunch of people to work with and work for. One of my best memories was when I flew the flight simulator. We discovered I am definitely not pilot material—I flew my plane through buildings and trees. Laughing, the pilots draped one of their scarfs around my neck despite my incompetence.

Joe wanted to branch out to a different field and made the decision to cross train to become a Loadmaster on the C-141's assigned to Norton AFB in San Bernardino, California. This change of career necessitated a move, so off we went back to California. This meant we were a lot closer to his mother and my family in San Diego. I was ecstatic.

We chose to live in the northern part of San Bernardino, near the San Bernardino mountains and approximately 25 miles from Big Bear. I had a need to be closer to nature versus city life but couldn't explain why. Lilies lined the driveway of our first rented home. This is where Little Joe learned the manly art of peeing in the bushes—thanks Joe/dad. Our oversized backyard was home to Easter egg hunts, and Dominic, my nephew, helped us hide eggs that may still live in that backyard. Victoria said her first sentence when she saw our vinyl Santa listing on our front door—"Santa fall off door." at least 20 times.

I was still active as a civil service employee and transferred to Norton AFB, into the civilian personnel office. Over time I was promoted through the ranks ultimately becoming a Personnelist within this office. I met my dear friend, Karen, there. We worked closely together until Norton AFB was closed in 1992. I found I was defining myself through my employment, especially since gaining knowledge and skill in the civilian personnel field helped me climb this ladder of success.

Joe was gone a lot. His job was a Loadmaster on the C-141, a cargo plane. A simplified explanation of his duties was he ensured whatever cargo they were moving was balanced so the plane wouldn't crash. In any given month he was home about seven days and the remaining 21-24 days he was gone.

As a military spouse, I kept the home fires burning while trying to achieve my personal goals. I adopted the goal to obtain my bachelor's degree along with most of the other civil service employees. Higher education equaled better promotion opportunities. Psychology became my major for the same reason.

I spread myself thin being both mom and dad, working full-time, and being a full-time student. When the children were small it was easy to parent. I tried to make sure we had quality time when we were together—every Friday night we'd have McDonald's and go to the movies at the base theater. However, the guilt for leaving them in childcare was a daily heartache. I felt I was not being a good mom. In order to survive and carry on, I buried my feelings.

Life was fairly smooth when they were young. I was able to allow the beginnings of my true self to emerge. The conviction I was a storyteller grew with each book I read. I began one tale with a female protagonist (major character) finding her true purpose, I attended writing classes and did research. I was creating another world, and I was excited.

Soon the children were growing older and had more interests and needs. Keeping the children involved in activities was a strategy so they wouldn't notice Joe wasn't home. They played soccer and loved it. I fulfilled my role and became the team's soccer mom. Then the movie Troop Beverly Hills aired, and Victoria wanted me to be her troop leader. As a former Girl Scout, it was a natural conclusion I'd be her Girl Scout leader. Reflecting back on this, I think volunteerism was an addiction for me—I had to prove I was worthy.

I kept adding more and more responsibilities to my plate, and soon there wasn't enough time to work on my novel. My self-limiting beliefs reared their head again undermining my confidence and reinforcing the idea it was selfish to put myself before my family.

In 1989 the Base Realignment and Closure (BRAC) commission placed Norton AFB on the Department of Defense base closure list for a variety of reasons. It was time for us to move again. We headed north to Washington state and McChord AFB. It was time for me to look for a new job and get re-established within a new social structure. This was more complicated as the children were in elementary school and needed to do the same.

We arrived at McChord AFB in December 1991. We stayed at temporary lodging, a little two-bedroom house, while we were house hunting. In the unit next to us, another couple arrived with their baby girl. Beth, the mom, and I liked each other on the spot. Neither of us realized we'd develop a lasting friendship spanning over 25 years and counting.

Joe and I focused our house hunting in the Puyallup School District area. We were told the quality of their academics, teachers, and culture of caring was where we wanted to place Joe, Jr. and Victoria. Joe, Jr. entered 4th grade and Victoria was in 2nd. Their time in elementary school was great. Again, I kept them occupied in soccer, and I became Victoria's Girl Scout leader again until she was in 4th grade.

Joe was still averaging seven days a month at home—his Air Force commitment had him in the field. I tried to be there for the children, but they were growing up, wanting their independence, and I tried to keep pace with them.

It was when they grew into teenagers I began to struggle. My parenting style wasn't effective because it was fear-based. I was raised with the understanding you tried your best in school, be respectful to the teachers who were authority figures, and you had passing grades—always striving for A's. I tried to force this belief upon Joe, Jr. and Victoria, and they didn't want any part of it.

I was afraid they'd opt for drugs when offered. I was appalled when I was told Joe Jr.'s 8th grade class was the worse for drug use to date. I kept too close an eye on their behavior and possibly forced them to keep too many secrets from me.

I alienated my teens, and I didn't have anyone to turn to for help. It was a universal expectation you didn't reach out to anyone connected with the military for help, such as a mental health counselor. It was paramount that none of this leaked back to Joe's commanding officer and potentially have a negative effect on his career. It didn't help I was conditioned to believe my only option to receive assistance with my struggles was to have a military health care provider.

I kept believing I should be able to control this situation because I was a teen once. I could see Joe, Jr. and Victoria's success in my mind's eye, and I wanted them to see their future, too. I pushed hard, and they pushed back. They wanted, and should have been allowed, to grow up and be independent souls. Joe and I became the authority figures my children aimed to thwart.

My philosophy was and still is their job was school and to do their best. However, I didn't factor in the social aspect they were exposed to. They didn't blend in—their coloring was striking with black hair, olive toned skin, and light brown eyes. They identified more with the other children of color in their school—which were not many. For whatever reason, it didn't affect them as much in elementary as it did when they entered secondary school.

Joe, Jr. fared well emotionally. Victoria struggled.

I was alarmed to find Victoria crawling to the bathroom when I came home from work. She looked up at me when I asked her what she had done. She said, "I took a lot of Tylenol". Panicked I asked her how many she took. In a slow and deliberate way as if her mouth couldn't form the words, she said she didn't know.

I don't know how we arrived at the hospital. I looked down on her in the hospital bed, hooked to an IV, and I was right back with Oba-chan as she laid dying so many years before. My heart skipped a beat, and I couldn't breathe. My baby girl's body was fighting the influx of acetaminophen, the life-threatening Tylenol poisoning.

I stroked her hair and murmured words of love, prayers, and encouragement. I told her to fight. I can't lose you. She had so much to live for. She laid there almost as white as the pillowcase and sheet that covered her.

The nurse came into the room to do a medical procedure, but I was focused on Victoria. The nurse leaned near me whispering "thank you" in my ear. Confused, I looked at her questioningly. She said all the other parents yelled at their children for attempting suicide. I was flummoxed. Why would parents do such a thing?

Things started to look dire as medical staff activity increased in Victoria's room. The doctors called for a helicopter transport to Harborview in Seattle for an emergency liver transplant. Panicked, I called my sister, Daelene, and her boyfriend, Art. Art did all the leg work in contacting Joe, who was in New Zealand, and started the process to get him home.

Before the helicopter was to arrive, they retested Victoria's liver enzymes.

They came back normal.

Yes, normal, as if the suicide attempt never happened. All of us are still bewildered by their findings—we can't figure out how they returned to normal.

I don't know if my response to this miracle intimidated her. I told Victoria God had a purpose for her, and I felt she needed to embrace it.

Victoria's choices spiraled out of control over the next four months. She made another suicide attempt with Tylenol. I thought I had removed all of it from the house, but I hadn't. I didn't know to look in all the nooks and crannies in the house. This time she went to Madigan Army Medical Hospital. Again, I don't know how we made it there. My mind and spirit reverted to the previous hospital that had treated her. Was this a form of PTSD?

Her medical team was able to treat her effectively, and she was stabilized. However, they wouldn't release her unless she went to inpatient treatment.

Joe and I chose for her to be transferred to Intermountain Hospital in Idaho. Treatment was hard for her and for us as well. The entire time I felt I failed her. While at Intermountain, Victoria made it clear to everyone she did not want to be there. But there she stayed and continued with all the treatment they offered.

In May 1998, my parents called and told me to come to their house. I met both my sisters, Daelene and Donnette, and their respective spouses there. From the charged energy flowing around us, I knew it was something bad.

"Your brother is dead." I don't know whether dad or mom told us. I believe it was dad as I can't imagine mom being able to utter the words.

I collapsed into one of the dining room chairs. This wasn't real. It had to be a lie.

I looked at my dad, and knew it was true. I lost awareness of my sisters, and I was hyper focused on my parents. My dad told us my brother's landlord discovered his body on May 26th.

A heaviness descended over me; energy drained from my pores. I couldn't focus. I couldn't think. My eyelids closed of their own accord. I mumbled something to the family and stumbled into my parent's spare bedroom. I lurched and fell onto the bed. A moment later I was asleep and stayed in that position for three hours. Shock had overtaken me.

My sisters and I, with our spouses, flew down to Escondido, California to clear out my brother's room and storage unit. We wouldn't let our parents accompany us—it simply didn't make sense. His room bore evidence of emergency personnel working on my brother and then removing him from the bedroom he had occupied for decades. But the disarray was a combination of Michael's hoarding as much as it was from the officials doing their job.

A numbness flowed over me. I looked at his empty bed and it registered he was really gone. I couldn't process what I was seeing in Michael's room. Stuff covered the furniture and floor—electronics, VHS tapes, and clothes. But the most disturbing was the small nasal inhaler tubes that littered the floor. They were everywhere. My focus narrowed upon them and I knew he had been inhaling them to get high.

I spun on my feet turning to look at a pile of papers. A familiar writing caught my attention. It was my letters to Michael. My breathing slowed—they were all unopened. The room receded and I was caught in a whirl of pain. I had shared of my life, of Joe, Jr.'s and Victoria's school pictures, and he hadn't opened them. Grief over the loss of my brother in my life was now intermingled with pain and anger of this rejection.

We were still days away from the memorial service arranged by Michael's coworkers and boss, so the six of us went to clear out his storage unit. We walked in and couldn't move forward. It felt like a tornado had dumped debris into this small space. The most profound thing was the sheer number of TV Guides Michael had saved—he had at least a decade's worth of the weekly magazine. This more than anything demonstrated his obsessive compulsiveness. We bagged all the items with little or no value for the trash and kept sentimental items for our family.

What I brought home in remembrance of my big brother was his guitar. He played Beatles songs all the time and this sparked my love of the band. I remember when he tried to teach me to play and my fingers and hands were too small to play the different chords. There were other mementos I kept, but I don't remember what my sisters brought home.

It took us a week to clear out his room and storage unit, and the memorial service was held the day before we flew back to Washington. At the service, his coworkers spoke with love for my brother. They called him the Gentle Giant. Daisies were carried by most people; they were Michael's favorite flower.

Michael's death certificate and autopsy report were mailed to my parent's home. When I read it, I was shocked to see he had passed away two days before his body had been found, and the inhaler cotton wicks were found in his stomach. I couldn't stop the flow of emotions and visions that crossed my mind. He died alone after ingesting the wicks. My heart sank at the thought of him possibly reaching for help, but not having the ability to call out. I tormented myself with the thoughts of how long it took him to die, of what pain he had in his life he had to eat the cotton to drown it out, and that I had been celebrating my birthday when he had died.

My sisters and I planned Michael's memorial service at Daelene's church in Yelm. It was to be held in July. The loss of Michael was so acute it wouldn't be right if Victoria couldn't attend. Joe and I made the decision to bring her home for the service.

The decision to bring her home for the memorial was right. The decision to not take her back to Intermountain Hospital was wrong. I had missed her so much. Michael's loss was in every thought I had, and the thought of losing another loved one albeit to another state was too much to bear. Joe didn't want her to go back either so we kept her home with us.

The first weeks after the memorial service we—Joe, Joe, Jr., Victoria, and I—loved on each other. We had hoped our lives would continue this way. However, little by little, Victoria's behavior reverted to where she had left off.

It appeared at some point she decided suicide wasn't the answer. Instead, she began to make poor life choices to escape from her reality. She turned to drugs and alcohol.

I lost my daughter to the choices she made. I lost touch with my son because I was hyper focused on his sister. Deep in my heart I knew I was a horrible mother.

Meanwhile, I continued to be the dutiful military spouse and kept the home fires burning. I kept everything about Victoria to myself, I kept working, I kept being mother and father, and I kept taking care of the house.

Wearing the mother label and wife label didn't leave time for me to wonder if I was living my truth. I didn't have to ponder this. If and when I fell asleep, it was deep and dreamless. More often, I was awake busily trying to fix what I didn't have the capacity to repair.

• • •

Another label we wear, often simultaneously, is *employee* and *boss*. I chose to wear this label as a badge of honor. I needed to feel achievement in my career in contrast to feeling like a failure in my personal life.

In my eyes it was clearly my fault Victoria attempted suicide the first time. Somehow, I failed her. I didn't see the *help me* signs she was sending out. This belief stayed with me for years—for half a decade. In my attempt to be there for her, I quit my job to stay home with her. I thought it was a sensible plan, but she didn't think so. She continued to run away for weeks at a time, hanging out with other kids who were runaways. It was after she was in her late twenties when I found out adults were harboring her. If I had known at the time, someone would have gone to jail. I had called the morgue, hospitals, and all the friends she used to run with. I couldn't find her. I couldn't sleep, I was always on edge, and guilt was eating away at me.

Victoria would eventually show up around the three-week mark as if nothing happened. Joe and I would put her on restriction. She'd stay home for the restriction, but once it was over, she was a runaway, again.

The authorities wouldn't help us. The school said she'd go to juvenile detention for missing so much school, and Joe and I would be fined as we were responsible for her. After years of living this way, Joe and I finally accepted she would come home when she needed something, and we'd keep her home by putting her on restriction. We didn't see any other way of reaching her. I gave her to God and prayed for her every night.

I wanted to make a difference in a child's life since it seemed I couldn't make a difference in Victoria's. The pivotal point for the children in our area seemed to be in 5th and 6th grade. I brainstormed where I could provide a positive impact to children which didn't require a counselor's credentials. That's when I noticed the preschool and child-care center located in our neighborhood.

I stopped one day and applied for a position. I was hired almost immediately as a School Age Teacher. I didn't understand the industry, but it didn't matter. The pay was low, the responsibility high, but it was rewarding to make a positive difference in a child's life.

I fell in love with the kids. I could see I was making a positive impact by being genuinely interested in them as people. The activities we explored, arts and crafts, science, and other areas including outdoor time helped build a bond between me, a trusted adult, and the children. Summers and holidays were the best times as I was able to take them on field trips.

I believed this job helped ease the pain I was feeling at losing Victoria. I was wrong—it was another layer over the pain.

Events in all our lives overlap. It was true with my family and my work life. Dad began to have seizures and was taken to the hospital by ambulance. The doctors couldn't identify what was going on and released him. He had gone to the hospital at least twice in October 1998.

Another seizure hospitalized him in early November. My sisters, my mom, and I were in the waiting room anticipating news from the doctor. The nurse came out and ushered us into a small room. I knew something was off, but I couldn't figure out what. The doctor came in and told us dad had three golf ball sized tumors in his brain.

Everything after he said this was a blur. My mind was reeling. The how's and why's were whipping around in my brain. What did penetrate was the doctor saying dad didn't have a lot of time left.

Dad began chemotherapy and radiation treatment. He lost his hair, but he didn't lose his sharp sense of humor and wit. Over time, I could see him losing some of his energy as the treatment continued. Being sick all the time took a toll on him.

Dad was hospitalized for the last time on Christmas Eve, 1998. Mom and I sat in his room willing him to live. I had reached out to my sisters, but they couldn't make it so soon. They had to travel to be here, and I knew they would miss his passing.

Logically, I understand why a DNR is written. It's for the benefit of the person, as it should be. But I was raging inside—I wanted the nurses to do something, but they couldn't. Time slowed and nothing was being done for him. He wasn't on oxygen, he had pain meds to keep him comfortable, but I could feel him slipping away from me.

At noon, dad flat-lined. I jumped out of my chair as mom reached for me. I wasn't going to let him die.

I was going to pound on his chest to make his heart start beating again.

The two nurses came at me widening their stance to block me from reaching dad's hospital bed. This was my daddy dying. My hero. He could not die. I was ready to take them on.

As I eyed them an unexpected calm descended over me, and suddenly I could see this from my dad's perspective. He had been in pain for months. He had not been himself. He was ready to go home. Who was I to try to stop his passing? It would only be for my benefit. I knew he'd live in my heart forever, but there was still a part of me who wanted him to be here in the flesh.

I had to wait until the 26th to have my Dad's tribute inked into my skin. The pain of the needle as the tattoo artist created the cross, Daddy, and 12-24-98 in my skin never touched the depth of pain I felt at losing my father.

I jumped in my seat when the 21-gun salute commenced even though I knew it was coming. The deep bagpipe tones of Amazing Grace gave me chills. My mom, my sisters, and I sat in the front row being honored for my dad. His brown wooden urn sat on the table in front of us. I kept staring at it, the more I stared the more I wanted to jump up, grab it, and run away with it. He didn't belong in the niche they readied for him. I sat on my hands so I wouldn't get up.

Dad was interred at Tahoma National Cemetery along with our family dog, Duchess.

Meanwhile the Earth kept turning, everyone still conducted their business, and children must be cared for. What shattered my world had no bearing on my activities of daily living. I still needed to work, pay my bills, and otherwise function.

During my first six months working at the preschool and childcare center it was put on the closure list, and the director position became vacant. No one was applying for the position through the district or from the facility. After a lot of reflection, I decided to apply. Whether no one wanted to take over a closing childcare facility, or I was the only candidate, I was selected as director.

I was a workaholic with a dedication close to perfectionism. My official hours were 9 to 6, but I was up before the center opened at 5:30 a.m. and was at the center long after it closed. I was creating and implementing plans to share the value we gave to the families and children. They, in turn, brought us more families via word of mouth. I was enhancing our facility with information centers which were appealing and informative. I was growing our staff as our center was increasing in the number of children we served.

All these activities ensured closure was no longer an inevitable conclusion, and I went from supervising 11 staff members to 27. To sustain this growth and support my staff and children, I fell into a repeated habit of working six days a week at the center and seven days a week at home to the exclusion of a now empty house. I didn't want to face the fact I was an empty nester and my husband was gone all the time.

I filled my waking hours, and even extended my waking hours, with running my center. I never noticed I had a hole in my heart.

• • •

Some of us wear the label of *parents' caretaker*. We are also known as the Sandwich Generation as we are sandwiched between caring for parents and for our children. I wear the same label—I am my mother's caretaker.

After dad passed, mom continued living in their one-story home by herself. I was obsessed with running my center, so I rarely visited her. All seemed to be ok, but she began falling and hurting herself.

My sisters, my mom, and I decided mom couldn't live by herself anymore. It seemed logical she'd move in with me as we lived in the same town. I spoke with Joe and he agreed. We needed to buy another home that allowed mom to live on one level; we currently lived in a two-story where all the bedrooms were upstairs.

By 2002, mom moved in with us. We had purchased a split-level home with a gorgeous view of Mount Rainier. There were three bedrooms on the top level, two baths, the kitchen and dining room, and the living room. Mom would be able to have her bedroom, a sitting room, and her own bathroom. It was ideal.

I still didn't spend much time with her as I was continuing to work the same number of hours at the center. I don't know if that contributed to her decline.

In 2003, Joe retired from the Air Force. Victoria had been living with us since she turned 18 in 2002.

Victoria became pregnant and gave birth to her son, Jasper, in May 2003. Jasper's daddy, Keith, moved into the basement with her. It was about this time Joe, Jr. moved in with his girlfriend, Emma.

In September 2004, Victoria gave birth to her daughter, Juliet.

In early December 2004, Victoria and Keith were married. All were living in our basement.

In December 2004, mom called me when I was hosting our annual winter program at the childcare center. She told me she had fallen. I turned over the event to one of my staff and rushed home.

The doctor told me she had shattered her hip when she fell and would need hip replacement surgery. I felt horrible and guilty that I hadn't been home for her. After surgery, she went to a nursing home for four months for rehabilitation.

Joe and I talked about mom. He had started working for the railroad at that point, and we decided I could stay home and take care of her. It would be too difficult to run a preschool and childcare center and take care of her at the same time.

In April 2005, I became mom's caretaker. I had to coax her to come out of her room to eat her meals. Her physical therapist wanted her walking to increase her mobility and range of motion. It was too easy for mom to immobilize and isolate herself. I believe the self-isolation was a genetic issue we all shared. Mom and my brother, Michael, were examples of this. I know I have the tendency to self-isolate if I don't leave the house at least once every two days. I believe Daelene and Donnette have the same tendency.

I'd push mom to walk around the house and to take herself to the bathroom. She would get angry with me and told me I was punishing her. I kept explaining it was for her own good. I was fighting a losing battle.

Meanwhile, Victoria, Keith, Jasper, and Juliet were living in the basement of our house. There were three bedrooms, a bathroom, a workshop, and family room in the basement with a separate entrance.

When Victoria and Keith wanted to go out, I'd take care of Jasper and Juliet. Their return times became later and later until finally they were gone for days. I told them I couldn't watch the babies while I was taking care of grandma. They didn't listen and disappeared for weeks at a time leaving me alone with mom, and the babies. Joe's schedule with the railroad had him gone for three days and back for 12 hours, sometimes eight. It was whatever the railroad wanted him to do.

I was frustrated, trapped, and angry, but was afraid to voice it. And even if I could voice it, who would I tell it to? I was 45 years old and this was supposed to be my time to explore who I was, and I couldn't. I was caring for my mother and my two grandchildren.

This was my new reality.

• • •

Another label which is becoming more prevalent is *grandchildren's caretaker*. Some of us are the *Hero Sandwich Generation*; we are caregivers for our grandchildren and our parents.

It's June 2005 now, and I am mama and papa to Jasper, 24 months, and Juliet, 9 months. Victoria and Keith were rarely at the house. Joe had to follow the railroad's work demands and was gone a lot.

It hit me; I am responsible for both babies. My heart raced, I felt flushed, and my anxiety rose. I wouldn't be able to get them medical care without one of their parents being there. What would I do if one of them got hurt? One was a toddler and the other was moving right on up behind her big brother. Exploring their space, their environment would inevitably bring injuries. I had to be able to get them medical care. All those thoughts raced through my mind.

Joe was concerned, too. We had to gain the legal right to care for them and not only be stand-in babysitters. We discussed our next steps and agreed we'd petition the court for legal guardianship in July 2005.

The judge looked at us and basically said 'This is not how we normally do things. CPS presents the case and we place the children with you." I didn't know how to respond. I thought, why would we wait for CPS to be involved and have the children be more traumatized?

In February 2006, the judge granted us temporary legal guardianship until Jasper and Juliet reached 18 years old. The processing of the case took longer than I had hoped, but luckily neither one needed medical care during that time. Joe and I expected Victoria and Keith to heal themselves and regain custody of their children in one year.

Mom's descent into dementia added another level of energy I had to navigate. She viewed Jasper as an adversary in our family dynamics. If Jasper gained my attention, whether positive or negative, mom would do something, again positive or negative, to direct it towards herself. She made a point of squabbling with Jasper every day. She said he was getting in her way when she was exercising with her walker. I secretly laughed because this is what motivated her to walk.

Several times I caught mom chasing Jasper around the dining room and kitchen. Jasper skipped backward to keep mom in sight; a constant giggle escaped him. Mom leaned her upper body over her walker like it gave her an advantage, her face was determined—I knew she would run him over if he tripped.

Life became more stressful. I had three in diapers. Being in diapers meant nothing to the two younger ones. Mom was upset about it. There was a part of her who believed it shouldn't be that way. Her choices to rebel were limited, but she found effective ways to let me know she wasn't happy.

I made meals for three different eating abilities. I had to be conscious of swallowing hazards for all three of them. I had to be mindful of the texture and softness of the food, especially for mom. She let me know when the spaghetti noodles were too firm for her liking by throwing them at me.

This was not my mom. This was my mom's body consumed by dementia. Sadly, I didn't recognize this until years after she passed.

On top of it all, I had to manage the household—paying bills, cleaning, grocery shopping—all the day-to-day things everyone does. Thankfully, Joe took care of the yard work and car maintenance.

The stress of being the go-to person for all three of them took its toll on me. I wasn't sleeping well, I was fatigued, and I was grumpy. I reached out to my sisters and we discussed the dysfunction in my household. We decided mom would be better served in an assisted living facility which would offer the skilled care I couldn't provide.

And with this additional label of grandchildren's caretaker, I am no closer to knowing who I am, or what my truth is.

Catalyst for change.

My sisters and I transitioned mom to an assisted living facility Donnette found in Lacey where she lived. The facility was several stories high, and mom's room was on the second floor. All three of us unloaded her boxes and furniture and arranged it for her. We stayed with her and visited the different areas, so she'd feel comfortable. We went to the dining hall, to the lobby where some of the activities were done, and to the station where the staff were.

I know my sisters explained to mom this transition was for her best interests. They'd have staff available to help her during the night and day. She didn't believe them anymore than she believed me. I felt she held me responsible for this move.

I carried the guilt of putting her in the facility for years. It was a sharp pain in my heart that I couldn't ignore. I live with this guilt less frequently now, but all of it makes me sad.

Mom refused to socialize with anyone at the facility. She ate in her room and declined all interest in bingo, card games, and craft activities. Not only did she isolate herself, but she lost much of her mobility because she wasn't going downstairs to participate.

Jasper, Juliet, and I would travel to Lacey and visit mom occasionally. The kids would love on her, and she welcomed it. Whatever caused the friction between Jasper and mom, was gone. Our visits would be short as the drive was over an hour.

Over the course of several years, her health deteriorated, and she was moved to a nursing home. I believe she lost her will to live. I'm not sure if it was due to depression over her surroundings, or if her heart was broken over losing dad, or a combination of both.

In the summer of 2008, mom was transported to hospice in University Place, which was closer to me. We entered the one-story building to help settle mom in. The staff greeted us with calm, quiet demeanors and energy. They were respectful and gentle of mom and of us.

They let us know when mom's time was growing close. Daelene, Donnette, Jasper, Juliet, and I spent the night on August 28th keeping vigil over her.

Early on August 29th, without a sound mom went home to join dad. The hospice staff entered her room solemnly, noiselessly and removed all the medical equipment. They brought the quilt and blankets up to her chin, tucking her in, so she appeared to be sleeping. They disappeared as we all gathered around mom's bed.

My heart broke for the loss of my mother. A fragment of my mother existed when dementia took over. I was lost in the battle of living in the now, of keeping the squabbling down, of caretaking the shell of my mother, of giving the children some normalcy so they wouldn't notice their parents weren't there, of maintaining Joe's and my household, of giving and not receiving, that I didn't *see* her.

Now, mom was gone, and I couldn't mend the fences that were broken and untended all those decades. I grieved for my loss, for Jasper and Juliet's loss of knowing their Oba-chan, and of my sisters' loss as we became orphans that August day.

Losing mom was the fourth most painful event I experienced; the first was losing my Oba-Chan, then Michael, and then my dad.

Mom's death was the catalyst for change in my life. She stopped living her life when she moved into my house. Or was I more aware of it and she had truly stopped living when dad passed away? I'm not sure, but I do know for at least eight years she did not really live even though she physically existed with us.

There are many of us who exist as a resource for others within our lives. We are the parent to their child. We are the spouse. We are grandparents raising grandchildren. We are employees or bosses.

But who are we really? Who is that in your mirror? Do you know who looks back at you? I didn't.

I was 48 when mom passed away. I believed the way she lived the last years of her life was the stimulus for me to examine my own life. I needed to know who I truly was. Was I all the labels I had been wearing for the last 40 years? I needed to know.

And so, the journey begins.

CHAPTER 6

FACE YOUR REALITY

See yourself in the mirror for who you truly are—love each imperfection which makes the perfect you.

Are you living your truth?

Or are you living your truth as defined by someone else?

If you're living your truth, how many people tried to stop you?

I found without defining the core of who I was, I would run and jump from label to label. Sometimes I found I was wearing different ones at the same time. I'd be employee, daughter, and mother. I'd question myself-was this really me? The answer is yes and no at the same time. I was part of one label or maybe I was all of them, then my core would waver like a flag in the wind.

I was a volunteer Girl Scout leader. Once I had mastered all that meant I had a need to do more. I volunteered for more positions in the Service Unit—managing calendars and cookies, but still maintaining the troop for Victoria. I never felt complete, that I had done enough, so I needed to do more. I believed I needed to define my epicenter, my identity, so it would anchor these labels together.

When mom passed, I realized I had been knowingly living other people's expectations, and I was totally unaware that I adopted their belief systems at the same time. I wasn't living my truth; discontent was my underlying constant companion. I tried to become who I was meant to be, but I allowed society's stereotypical definitions to keep me in a prison of my own making and it chafed.

Reflection #1: Facing My Reality—Self-Limiting Beliefs.

Since the age of 22, I've dreamt of becoming an author. I started and stopped several novels over these 30 plus years. Each novel had a female protagonist who is either looking for her identity, or her destiny/identity is revealed to her. I'd reach the point in the storytelling where she was on the verge of discovery and found I couldn't finish the book. Either the story withered away, I had writer's block, or I allowed my life to overtake me.

I realize now I allowed self-limiting beliefs to pull me away from my dream of writing because I didn't consider myself important enough to expect equal time in our family. I believed all my time should be dedicated to the children, my spouse, and our home. This was my learned behavior from my parents. How did my choice help my children?

Also, I believed I was to keep the home fires burning while my military spouse was gone most of the month, every month. He had the more important job. He was serving our country, and my job was to make it easier for him by ensuring everything flowed smoothly and calmly at home. This was not his expectation, but he didn't dissuade me from doing it.

I was working a full-time job that I dedicated myself to. To perform less than the full extent of my skills was to dishonor my father. Did dad tell me this? No. This was something I told myself. However, my father's work ethics were clearly defined. Whatever your *work* was (school or a job) you gave your all, you were always on time, and you only called out sick if it was absolutely necessary. In one job, I was told the only way I'd call out was if I *called out dead.* This was how important my father's opinion was.

In my confused mind, I focused on what his work ethic was and therefore had to live up to it. In reality, dad would have never expected nor would want me to work to the exclusion of everything else in my life.

Reflection #2: Facing My Reality—Stifling My Truth.

I believe family secrets are a universal theme for everyone. In my family, this expectation began a long time ago, almost 100 years. My parents were born in the early to late 1920's. This was the Silent Generation for my father. This was where children were seen but not heard. My mother had the same restriction, and it came handed down to me and my siblings. Food for thought...what was handed down to you?

Also, authority figures have a special hold on us. They range from your parents, grandparents, teachers, spiritual leaders, doctors, and others. They were never questioned or disobeyed. Today, we have a different worldview of authority figures. We realize now these influencers are first human beings who are fallible. But being a child of the '60's and a girl, I held them in a higher regard and didn't question them. The telling of sexual abuse, then and now, is too sophisticated to share from a child's worldview. I didn't have the words to tell my parents and wouldn't know where to begin even if I had them.

Joe and I are from the same generation, so secret keeping wasn't new to us. Potential embarrassments were to be kept within the four walls of our home. I wasn't allowed to share even with family.

When Victoria was a tween she started experimenting with chemicals, attempted suicide, and almost died. I believed when she wasn't successful with ending her life, she started hanging out with people who lived on the edge and entered into unlawful behavior. She acted out and I tried to control her—fights between us would ensue. I kept it all to myself.

During one fight she picked up a bat. She was standing over four feet away from me, and she didn't intend to use it. She was using drugs, I was attempting to get her to the hospital, and she refused to go. In Washington state, children 13 and older make their own medical decisions. I made a call to the police for help explaining I wanted to get her to the hospital.

The sheriff's deputy who came to our house was a familiar face, and he wanted to help us. I explained I was trying to get Victoria to triage at the local hospital. He wrote up the report so strongly (meaning he exaggerated stating she was trying to kill me) the state's prosecuting attorney decided to use her as the example of teenage violence against parents. The deputy's plan backfired when the hospital refused to accept Victoria due to the level of violence she allegedly exhibited.

The prosecuting attorney charged her with a felony, and she went to jail. Joe and I bailed her out and hired an attorney to represent her. At the end of the proceedings, she was on deferred disposition, meaning she had to be *good* for a year, and the charges would go away. She was already a troubled teen, so the future didn't look hopeful.

I wrote up a victim's statement explaining how the sheriff deputy was attempting to help me but wasn't aware of the prosecuting attorney's agenda. The prosecuting attorney didn't pay any attention to it even when the judge cautioned him about it. He used my daughter as a springboard for his re-election capitalizing on the Thurston High School shooting in Springfield, Oregon. I didn't fight any of it.

I let myself be silenced because I was taught to be this way.

I own my choices. It is no one's fault but mine.

Now what?

Reflection #3: Facing My Reality—Following Society Dictates.

I belonged to several traditional churches over the years—exactly as my mom did. I tried to find comfort and belonging in each one, but I never *fit* in. As I grew older, I realized what was missing. They weren't accepting of other belief systems. This didn't mesh with me or my family dynamics. My grandmother was Buddhist, and my mother moved between different religions in the Christian faith because she couldn't find one which was tolerant of people's flaws. The myriad of people who inhabit the Earth with different faiths needed to be represented and respected and my own beliefs are spiritually eclectic, meaning I choose the tenants of different belief systems and adopt them as my own.

I wanted to belong to a spiritual body which accepted differing belief systems with the basic tenant of *Do No Harm*. At this point I wasn't sure such a spiritual body even existed, or what religious/spiritual umbrella it would fall under.

I kept looking for a church which met my needs, but it required more effort than I could produce. I fell into a pattern of belonging to churches which didn't resonate with me.

• • •

The goad, the event that roused me to act to face my reality, was the death of my mother. She had spent the last ten years of her life lost, marking time, and slowly dying of a broken heart.

I was 48 and had another lifetime to either mark time or to live. I chose to live. I chose to embrace my reality and find my purpose.

It was time to peel away the layers which had cocooned my core. It was time to become who I was meant to be.

My first step was to peel the outmost layers—my current physical, emotional, and mental state. I began reflecting on my marriage, and my relationship with Joe.

Joe and I lost each other in the process of parenting and life's other challenges. We forgot to nourish and love each other.

I accepted and understood why he had been away from us while he was active duty. He was serving a larger purpose he believed in, and I believed in it, too—Dad was retired Navy. Joe, Jr., Victoria, and I benefited from his service on a physical level. We had good medical care even if it came with conditions. Joe provided half of our income, and I wouldn't have visited Okinawa or England without him. Most of all, I wanted him to be happy.

Joe's first job after retiring was as a security officer on McChord AFB. It was a bit of a culture shock for him—it would be for me, too—as the office was without windows. It was overwhelming when one compared it to his previous career of flying to different locales for 18 years. But as a security officer, he came home every day, and I loved it.

I understood when he wanted to find another job where he could be outdoors. That environment suited him better than an office. What I didn't understand was why he chose another occupation that would take him away from his family. Logically, I understood his reasoning—the money would be good working for the railroad, job security was there if one learned how to navigate their bureaucracy, and he found this was the best possible way to take care of his family. But he didn't talk to me about it. He didn't explain he'd be working the *extra board*, meaning the trips would be leaving at different days and times with as little as eight hours off between shifts, at all hours of day or night.

I was angry he was gone all the time. I've never said that before. I always put on a brave front and put a positive spin on it. To admit I was lonely, felt rejected, felt I was taken for granted said I was ungrateful and selfish. With dad's and mom's belief system always in the back of mind, I could do nothing else but accept.

Communication wasn't one of our strengths. He would come home from a trip and immediately take the grandkids out. He thought he was giving me a break. I thought he was rejecting me. I never talked to him about it, and he never approached me, either.

Mom's death brought a clarity I had never known. She *existed* she didn't *live*. I wanted to live. I wanted to define who I truly was. I didn't want to be a character in someone else's dream.

Joe's goal was to have a house, wife, and children, and we'd live happily ever after. This was an honorable goal for him, but it wasn't mine. I didn't want to be a place holder in my own life. I wanted to find my purpose.

We continued to drift apart and disagree until our marriage dissolved.

Another step in facing my reality meant I would choose my career. This was a huge step for me, and I was excited. Over the years I was drawn to the healing field, and I wanted to be part of it. I prayed and meditated on what direction I should take. My self-limiting beliefs said I was too old for nursing, so I researched massage therapy.

I reached out to the instructors at a local technical college. They were honest and admitted to me that as I got older my body may not hold up, but there were many massage modalities to choose from.

At almost 50 years old, I was in massage school.

And this is the start of me living my authentic life.

PART THREE

Avoid the Mirror

INTRODUCTION TO PART THREE

AVOID YOUR MIRROR

"Pain in this life is not avoidable,
but the pain we create avoiding pain is avoidable."

— R.D. Laing

There are times we are totally clueless in the choices we make. This is where we avoid our mirror; we ignore our truth.

It took a lot of effort, strength, and determination to make the decision to live my authenticity.

In the next chapters, I share about one event, granted it was a large one, which sent me backward by leaps and bounds to live in my self-limiting beliefs. I had been conditioned for 50 years to live these beliefs, so one and a half years of living my purpose wasn't enough to stand strong against that conditioning.

CHAPTER 7

LIVE THEIR EXISTENCE

You've discovered your purpose and identity. Think critically, plan carefully, and move deliberately with trusted and like-minded advisors to avoid slipping back into your former shell.

One of the definitions of *manifest* found in the Encarta Webster's College Dictionary is "...to appear or be revealed...". To manifest your intention is a powerful tool. Oprah utilized the practice of manifestation to get where she is today. She visualized it and did the work behind it to create it in her life.

Are you able to attract what you want to create in your life?

It's one of those adages...*be careful what you wish for.*

I created these intentions.

I am resolute in expressing who I am.

I establish my goals.

I will write my book. I own my part in allowing my guilt and not feeling *good enough* to sabotage my writing dream. I claim my dream now.

I need a job to support the children and me while I'm writing my book.

I want the job to resonate with who I am. In years gone by, I allowed myself to bend with the wind. I applied for entry-level positions because I didn't feel qualified or *good enough.*

As you know, my desire to be of service lead me to massage therapy school but becoming a massage therapist wasn't the end goal.

Being employed in a healing profession with time off while the grandchildren were in school was. In addition, eighteen months of massage school doesn't lend itself to writing fiction. The two hemispheres of the brain do not work together. In simplest terms, one side is the analytical side and the other, the creative. In me, never the twain shall meet. I focused on my college courses because of the time limit I was under. If I was truthful, however, it was mostly because I doubted my talent as a writer.

I left the liquid sunshine (rain) and visited the real sunshine in San Diego several times while in massage school. The first time was for the 40th Homecoming of my high school in September 2010. This was the stimulus for many of the following events in my life.

Many alumni returned home to celebrate this once in a lifetime event. I caught up with dear girlfriends, my Ya-Ya's, and was reacquainted with Mike, an honorary Ya-Ya dubbed a Yo-Yo. Facebook's popularity was growing, and we took advantage of it to keep in touch in between my visits.

In December 2011, Jasper, Juliet, Daelene, and I went to San Diego. We visited Daelene's kids, saw my Ya-Ya's for the first ever cookie bake, and attended Grinch the musical. This is when the attraction between Mike and me began.

Mike was opening himself back up to the possibilities of a purposeful life, a journey I fully understood. His almost daily surfing under the California rays bronzed his skin. Mike's stocky frame resembled his father's, and his dedication to time spent with his mom, usually at bingo, endeared him to me. He moved back to San Diego to be with his family, and that was exactly what he was doing.

He and I talked daily learning and absorbing more about each other during the last months of my massage studies. There was no formal proclamation of us becoming boyfriend and girlfriend, it simply was.

It was during this period I realized it was time to move where my heart was. My heart was in southern California where I grew up. During my marriage, I never had a say in where we were living, but this was the life of a military spouse and we went where the Air Force sent us. But now, I could choose. I chose my *home*, I chose my boyfriend, and I chose happiness. Or did I?

It may sound simple, but a lot of manifesting and logistics needed to be accomplished— tentative move date established, and housing found and rented. I decided to move while the children were still young so it wouldn't be as traumatic for them to acclimate to their new surroundings.

Making decisions and movement of this magnitude can overwhelm one's psyche especially if you have decades of negative conditioning behind you. Then pile on anger and eagerness, and I was an emotional mess.

My sister, Daelene, and Joe, Jr didn't take the idea of my move well. Daelene was angry and distanced herself from me. I lost my sister through this decision—grief saturated me as if she had passed away, but it was worse. We had always joked we were twins, and we truly were in my heart. When I lost her, a piece of me wasted away and died. Joe, Jr. was just as angry. He demanded to know if I was taking Jasper and Juliet with me. No other words were shared between us. His body language and demeanor said it all. I didn't know it was possible to lose more of myself, but the pain in my heart shredded me.

Today, I understand their anger. I upended their life—I was taking away part of their world. They didn't want it to happen and they were helpless to stop it. I was too shaken and confused then to process how they were feeling, let alone help them.

I flew to San Diego in the spring of 2012 so Mike and I could start the process of our life together. We house hunted and found an ideal rental property in Chula Vista. It was a two-story and in a good neighborhood for the children, and it had a 4th bedroom where I could massage. It was further away from the beach than Mike would've liked, but he didn't demur. We put down a deposit and opened a checking account together. His joy and eagerness were evident in all we did. My excitement overlaid the uneasiness I experienced; the result was a sickly sensation in my gut.

When I returned to Washington, the actions I put into play became real; I panicked. What the hell was I doing? Moving thousands of miles away? I had a support system here—friends I've interacted with for decades, friends and family to help with Jasper and Juliet and a job to support myself and the kids.

It was tearing a hole in my stomach. I wasn't sleeping, I couldn't eat. Anxiety was my constant companion. I was uprooting not only me but my grandchildren as well. I couldn't do it. I couldn't make the move to San Diego. I didn't know how to tell Mike but knew it had to be done and soon.

Daelene, Emma, my daughter-in-law, and I had a pre-planned trip to Forks, Washington, after I returned from San Diego. As we walked through Forks, I dipped into an alley to call Mike.

I felt like scum, a bottom feeder when I told him. He was stunned and hurt. I can't describe the pain he felt, but he told me he had no choice but to accept my decision. There was literally nothing he could do. He acted to end the lease, and the landlord understood. Mike thanked me, something I never expected, as my decision prodded him on his path. But that is Mike's way—to find the positive in any situation no matter how distressing.

The next reality hit me—I was a failure. I gave into my fear of the unknown and stayed in Washington like a coward. I sunk into a deep depression. One saving grace was my boss hadn't filled my massage position yet, so I was able to go back to work. I had a reason to get up in the morning. The pit at the bottom of my stomach went away, however, sleep still evaded me as did my appetite. I couldn't generate emotion—all my feelings had dulled. I was part of the walking dead.

I woke, took care of the kids, went to work, came home, took care of the kids, went to bed then repeated it all again. I did this for two months—living a zombie existence. A close friend looked at me and said in disgust, 'Why are you still here? Move already.'

I was stagnant and miserable here. I needed to face my fears and move. Otherwise, I knew I'd regret it for the rest of my life. I approached the move with determination and stamped out the fear the best I could.

I made another quick trip to San Diego and found a three-bedroom apartment for me, Jasper, and Juliet. One of my Ya-Ya friends, Debi, helped me finalize the paperwork for the apartment. I picked mid-December as our move date so the kids would have a couple of days with new school friends before winter break began.

Jasper and Juliet helped with packing. Before long we had built a small fort with all the boxes we would be shipping. As more boxes filled the living room, the sadder I was. This was the culmination of a 30+ year marriage. I was sad for the loss of it all. Joe and I did have love once, we had good times, and we made two beautiful children together.

As the move date loomed closer, Victoria told me she was coming with us. I was taken aback. She told me she wanted a new start, to get away from Washington. This I understood well. This would be a new beginning for her, and I couldn't leave her behind. Victoria added her boxes, and our fort became exponentially larger in more ways than merely physical belongings.

The movers arrived. I was equally happy and blue as I watched our boxes being whisked into their semi. I was literally and physically moments away from continuing my journey of self-discovery. But I was leaving my son, Joe, Jr., his wife, Emma, and my grandchildren Anthony, Marie, and Nicole, and my sisters behind. This tore at my soul.

Once the movers left, we jammed bags for three children and two adults along with our bodies into my

Kia Sorrento. Sadly, for everyone but me, I drove like my dad.

Dad was a focused driver; we only stopped for gas and that's when we all made a beeline to the restroom. When I stopped for gas, everyone got out of the car and made their own beeline to the bathroom or for snacks. Then it was on the road again. We made decent time which was good because I was determined to be there before the semi arrived.

We arrived at our *apartment home* which was the glorified name the apartment complex labeled our three-bedroom apartment. Mike met us there, and we moved in. Everything was as I manifested.

Then everything began to implode.

The self-limiting beliefs that budded when I said no to San Diego the first time dug their roots into my heart and spread like ivy. I worried about my ability to take care of the children, and myself financially. I convinced myself massage therapy was not a suitable career, and I needed to find one that offered retirement benefits, paid holidays, vacation, and sick time, Monday-Friday work—basically a traditional job.

For the first six months, I applied for any clerical jobs I could find. Again, I had forgotten my inner strength. The need to find job security was the first and foremost thing in my mind. The job didn't appear. I had dated office skills. Technology had advanced since the last time I worked in an office in 2005. Employers wanted someone with current office skills, so I enrolled at the local community college to become a desirable candidate.

Time slipped away. Winter turned to spring and no one in the apartment was particularly happy. I let anxiety build up in my heart and head. Self-limiting beliefs were the only thoughts I had. I couldn't get a job in the market I wanted, and I continued to hold myself to the clerical field believing it was the only answer. I went to screening tests, put myself on lists for employment, and went on a couple of interviews. None of these panned out.

Victoria was unhappy with San Diego. She didn't try to socialize. She self-isolated like her grandmother. I understood to a degree as her social anxiety was a family trait.

Summer was imminent, and I wanted the kids to be in Washington for their grandad's birthday and Father's Day. Victoria wanted to move back to Washington, and this was her opportunity. I went with them to help manage the children, but mostly to visit with my son and family, and my sisters.

We were at the airport getting ready to board, and one of my YaYa's, Mari, called me to tell me she had talked to her boss about a temporary hire. She networked a wonderful opportunity for me, and I will be forever grateful. I explained where I was and told Mari I'd reach out to her when I got back from my long weekend away.

Life became complicated a couple of weeks into the temporary position at Mari's office. I had applied for a position as an assistant director at a childcare center, Children's Wonder, before Mari called me, and they called and offered me the job.

I compared the opportunities. The assistant director position was closer to home, offered retirement, vacation and sick, and my income would increase significantly. The benefits of this position, especially being closer to the children, convinced me—I had no choice but to accept.

My days consisted of the commute and work, but the nights when the kids were gone were the hardest. I cried every night. This was the first time I had been alone with no one to take care of in ... oh my gosh, I've never been alone with no one to take care of in this sense. I had always been surrounded by family, and now I was alone except for the fish and frog in our aquarium.

I didn't know what to do with myself. I felt sad, lost, with an ache in my heart until I went to sleep, if sleep actually took me. Then it was time to wake and start the day all over again. Thankfully, they came home three weeks later. But I had a taste of being a true empty nester, and I had not been prepared.

For the next six months, I worked at Children's Wonder. Over time, I realized management's decisions were questionable and made me uncomfortable. I tried to make the best of it because, as always, the children were the best part of being in Early Childhood Education. Ultimately, I didn't find fulfillment there; I had lost my purpose. Jasper and Juliet weren't happy and let me know by their angry behavior at home. I spent all the quality time I could with them, which included breakfast at their elementary school, but I was still gone all day until early evening.

Mike was an important part of their life. He'd pick them up before daycare closed at 6 p.m. and took them swimming in his pool or to the beach. He fed them dinner often. Most of the time he took them to their football and cheerleading practices. Even Mike's mom would help with transportation for the kids when he couldn't do it. I appreciated all he did for my kids, but I still felt I should be doing these things.

Guilt overtook my life. Debi, and another Ya-Ya, Kali, also helped me by taking the kids to their practices.

Without them, and especially Mike, the kids would have missed out on extracurricular activities. I still believed I should be doing it all.

The energy between Mike and me became strained over time. I believed he harbored resentment towards me when I left him hanging from the previous attempted move. This was understandable. Our family dynamics was a culture shock for him and how time-consuming caring for my kids was. Mike didn't fully understand what it meant to be in the life of a relative raising children, children whose parents were afflicted by addiction and domestic violence.

Jasper had a hard time expressing his emotions in a healthy way. This had been going on since he was five. He'd focus his anger on me by hitting me. As he grew older, he'd continue to have outbursts, but the hitting stopped.

Now in San Diego, Jasper was angry at me. I put him in a school where he was bullied. He didn't know how to express his emotions, so I was the target of his resentment. Mike stepped in to stop the verbal abuse, his voice raised. Mike didn't like how it felt to be a disciplinarian or the fact he felt compelled to do it.

I told Mike about our family dysfunction before we moved, but it was so out of his world view he didn't fully comprehend what I meant. The realization hit only when he experienced it first-hand.

I believe Mike began distancing himself from me with verbal digs about my cooking, my sketching, and other things. He forgot Valentine's Day two months after the children and I arrived. This was a stark contrast to the celebrations of special days and *flowers simply because* when I lived in Washington. I buried my feelings as I was conditioned to do and began building a wall so he couldn't hurt me. Then in May, Mike gave me a surprise birthday dinner with some of the Ya-Ya's and their husbands. The wall melted, and I let my guard down.

My lease expired that same month, and I went to a month-to-month arrangement. I was waiting for Mike to tell me when his lease was up so we could look for a place together.

In July we were sitting at Lucky Waller Park waiting for the kids to finish their practices. The sun was shining, the skies were blue. It was a beautiful evening. I asked Mike about plans to find a place together. Without hesitation, he told me he renewed his lease weeks earlier because they offered him a bonus. He had never said anything to me, and he *knew* I was waiting on him.

This information laid between us like a dead fish. I didn't know what to say to him. My insides withdrew and curled upon itself. But I acted like this bombshell didn't affect me. I was good at hiding. That moment was surreal as we sat in the grass waiting on the kids.

I was rejected by my boyfriend. Today, I understand why life unfolded as it did. To help me with the children, Mike was now chained to mine. He didn't have the freedom to do as he pleased whenever he wanted. He was a babysitter, provided transportation, and refereed when the children fought. By the time I caught up with them I was exhausted. Time alone with each other was scarce. Two years prior, Mike had left a marriage that had him imprisoned for years, and now he was experiencing something similar. It didn't sit well with him.

Experiencing the children's behavior opened his eyes to a lifestyle he had never contemplated before. Abandonment, addiction, and domestic violence affected children in different ways. They weren't equipped to process these events and acted in the only ways known to them.

I felt I was a failure to the bone. My purpose was buried below the reality I lived in. I worked for a person with questionable ethics. I felt guilty Jasper and Juliet had to go to after school care although the woman who cared for them was kind and enjoyed them. I imposed on my friends to help me with the kids. Juliet was allergic to the sun. Jasper's behavior was out of control. My relationship was with a man I didn't know. I was headed for a breakdown, and I needed to get the kids back to Washington.

The Universe gave me harsh life lessons during the year I lived in San Diego:

- Manifestation (having your intentions come true) without mapping out the next step may backfire.
- You're playing with fire if you don't maintain your identity when you manifest. I was two different people during this chapter. The beginning of Chapter 7 I was stepping onto my path and living my truth. At the end of this chapter, I lived by society dictates making fear-based decisions.
- The Universe will give you what you believe.

With each *failure,* I retreated into learned negative behaviors without realizing it. Self-doubt overwhelmed me, and I lost sight of the mirror altogether.

Please be aware the recounting, processing, and finally understanding these events occurred over several years. Hind sight is truly 20/20.

CHAPTER 8

END MY LIFE?

Fear-based immobilization is a stranglehold on your life. Mindful movement is life fulfilling purpose.

There are two ways for your life to end. One is obvious. Death.

Death comes to us in many forms, as we all know. Accident, illness, natural causes, or by our own hand.

The other, in my opinion, is when we allow ourselves to *stay* where we are with no forward progress.

We end our life by staying at status quo.

Why stay at status quo? It could be because we aren't aware of anything else to strive for, because we're depressed, or because we're too afraid to try something new.

We are comfortable where we are and see no reason to change.

Or we could stay static because we're too afraid to step out of what society says is the norm. We've tried in the past and we were unsuccessful. The experience left us with zero confidence and unsure of our next step. We are immobilized by fear.

Does any of the above resonate with you?

• • •

As I laid on my couch in my rental in Spanaway, Washington, I couldn't generate the energy to get off it, let alone think. The move was successful, and Donnette was a big part of that. Once I started the ball rolling to move back, I went on autopilot, and Donnette guided me and helped pack me out.

Mike helped pack us out, too and was genuinely sad to see me leave. However, with his yo-yo behavior and his interpretation of mine, neither one of us knew where our relationship would go. As usual, I never called him out on how he treated me.

My self-esteem was non-existent. It was made clear to me in San Diego I couldn't live up to the expectations I put on myself. I couldn't find work in a field I believed was plentiful and would provide retirement, health and other benefits, and income to support my family. The job offer I did accept, on the surface, should have been ideal. From a leadership perspective, it was unprofessional. I couldn't be all things to Jasper and Juliet—breadwinner and 24/7 caretaker. The children's behavior ignited angry outbursts from all of us. Mike rejected me. How was Washington going to be different? The difference was Jasper and Juliet had family there.

The heaviness in my heart, body, and spirit immobilized me. It took effort to move my limbs. I wanted to lay on the couch and sleep. I wanted to sleep my life away.

I didn't consciously plan for the *after*. I was content in knowing the children had others to provide for them. I could remove the mantle of responsibility from my shoulders and transfer it to someone else.

The kids could live with their grandad, Joe. He would have to adjust his work schedule to accommodate this. I'd be dead, so he'd have to.[1]

Everything became a blur when Creator stepped in. I remember I talked to my childhood friend, Debi. Did I call her, or did she call me? My brain fog was too thick. What I do remember is Debi said she'd be on the next plane up here. The logical part of my brain kicked in—I am irresponsible if she flew here. I felt a glimmer of energy. I told her no; I was alright. It took time to convince her, but eventually the determination in my voice persuaded her. She was a God inspired human angel in my time of need.

The belief 'I would be ok' solidified in my mind as I convinced Debi, but I knew I needed help. Again, thank you Creator.

I hadn't established a doctor yet—we had just arrived. I reached out to my old doctor, Dr. Blackfield. Not only had he been my doctor, but he had been mom's doctor before she moved to assisted living in 2005. Our rapport was strong as it spanned over ten years. He listened to my concerns, took my input, and made decisions. He pulled strings to get me back into his patient schedule.

On New Year's Eve 2013, I sat in his office without animation, talking in monotones about what brought me in to see him. He wrote the prescription before I finished speaking. He told me to come back in one month or sooner if needed. On autopilot, I left his office and picked up my anti-depressants.

Deep inside I knew the pills weren't the total answer. But getting the chemicals balanced in my brain was the kick start I needed.

The analytical part of my brain was in control again. It suppressed my emotions, my creativity, and stifled my inner voice. I needed a job, and I needed to guide the children back on track. I needed order in my life.

I pursued a government job because this equated to retirement, security, and a schedule which would mirror Jasper and Juliet's. I scoured federal and state job boards daily. My resume was perfect, but I couldn't combat my physical age or the age of my skills. Again, I looked for entry-level positions, believing I was not *enough* to apply for positions commensurate with my knowledge, skills, and abilities.

I set myself up for another rejection by solely focusing on government employment. My depression deepened, but with the medication, I was able to mask my inner distress until Karen, my dear friend from Norton AFB, called to check up on me.

Our friendship spanned twenty-seven years. We always picked up where we left off as if no time had elapsed between phone calls or texts. I unloaded my story on her, and she shared in my pain. She invited me to stay with her in Colorado.

She buffered me, propped me up, and held my hand. She took me snowshoeing in Vail, and out to eat at a fantastic Mexican restaurant. More importantly, she let me sob and cry my heart out. She was another human angel coming to my aid. I will always be grateful to her.

I needed the time with her to begin my healing process. I needed to realize I couldn't drift back into the life I had before I left for San Diego. My family moved on and healed in my absence. I needed to align myself with their lifestyle now and develop mine. I needed to own my feelings and make changes to allow happiness back in my heart.

The long weekend ended before I knew it. I returned home with renewed resolve to live authentically, to own my reactions to events, to follow my path rather than what I believed society expected from me.

With a nudge from Creator, I posted on Facebook I was looking for a job. My former massage boss, Courtney, reached out to me saying she had an opening if I was ready to come back. The weight on my shoulders slid down my back as relief and eagerness filled me. She was my third human angel.

I was more than ready to join the team again. I renewed my credentials, and I seamlessly went back into the massage field. I kicked myself in the ass for having left it in the first place. When I left massage, I abandoned my authenticity, and I lived from a place of fear.

Employment was the last piece I needed in my survival foundation along with shelter, food, smooth transition for Jasper and Juliet, and my ability to cope with all that life was throwing at me. Even though I was walking on more level ground, I knew it wouldn't take much to knock me off my footing. I needed to add another layer to my base; I needed to reignite my spiritual life.

Before I left Washington, I was worshipping and learning about my spirituality alone. I shied away from organized religions especially with my experience at my last church.

I feel it's important to expose the children to different ways of believing, so we explored my last church. Jasper and Juliet enjoyed their Sunday School class, and

I was free to immerse myself in the service. From the first Sunday, I felt *off* as if something was missing. I pondered my feelings—the people were friendly, they greeted us warmly, the Pastor was the epitome of a religious leader, but I felt incomplete.

I prayed for guidance. Creator answered in a variety of ways—I was urged to explore all which made the kids and me unique. I reflected on Jasper and Juliet's native American heritage, my Japanese heritage and Buddhism, the Hawaiian influence on my mother as she was born and raised in Hawaii, and my own innate beliefs. I believe we are all energetically connected throughout the world: humans, animals, and the very Earth itself. I learned to weigh the viewpoints and principles of different belief systems and adopted those that resonated, that felt right, as my beliefs. This is the basis of my eclectic spirituality.

Armed with this knowledge I stopped attending the church—it wasn't a good fit for me. Several months passed before the pastor reached out to me and asked why I had been absent for so long.

"I've left the church." I told him.

He reasoned with me to stay. I don't know why I didn't tell him the reasons earlier, but I finally did. I told him with the multitude of people in the world, the different belief systems, and my basic belief we were all energetically connected that I needed to explore my spirituality.

Silence filled the airway for ten seconds or more, and he renewed his efforts to convince me to stay. I told him thank you, but no.

"You're going to Hell," he blurted out.

I don't know if the emotions in his tone were from disgust with me or if he was truly terrified for my soul. Whatever his intent, I felt personally attacked. At the time, I was scared, but now, more than ten years later, I realize he didn't represent everyone in his religion. It was his opinion and strong belief in his faith.

Solitary worshipping wasn't beneficial for me. I functioned alone in my heart and head for too long. I needed a community of like-minded people to support and who supported me. I knew of such a church and had wanted to attend prior to the San Diego move, but I made excuses not to go. I was too intimidated to attend alone.

Now, I forged ahead with the wisdom and desire to belong to such a body of people. I attended in the middle of 2014 and became a member in early 2015. Even with membership, I kept to myself without relationships developed with my fellow members. I still believed I wasn't good enough, and the children didn't want to attend. To avoid behavior outbursts, we escaped right after service was over.

Jasper and Juliet's choices upset the household from the time we moved back to Washington. Their way of coping was physically directed at each other or at me. We went into counseling with varying degrees of success. I can only guess at the cause; they each carried heavy weights from situations most children are not exposed to, and my depression may have triggered some of it as well.

We continued our forward motion through life, navigating behavioral issues, academic neglect, and the slow buildup of my patient base. At times we took two steps forward and was pushed back one. One of those times we were shoved back several feet.

The landlord of our rental property wanted me to buy it. It wasn't disclosed when we leased a major six-lane road would run through the housing area, and it would be located three houses away from where we lived. That wasn't my idea of a safe and quiet neighborhood, so I told them no.

The landlord responded by giving me 20 days to vacate.

Twenty days.

How was I supposed to find a home in the same school zone as the one we lived in? In the budget we could afford? And arrange for the actual move? How was I to rearrange my work schedule so my patients would still receive their treatment? Thanks to Courtney, time off was granted in a heartbeat. But how was I to accomplish the rest of it in 20 days?

My stress level went through the roof. I wilted under the pressure and curled up in bed and cried. This was too much, too soon—two years after we had moved from San Diego. The framework of who I was had been established, but I didn't know if it could withstand this kind of pressure.

My crying dried up. I felt Creator's touch, along with my angels and guides-not only could I do it, I would do it. I didn't have the luxury of falling apart. Two children and one cat, Freya, depended on me to get myself together.

I found a rental in the same school zone almost immediately although it was a little higher rent. I didn't have an option but to apply for it. We were accepted right away and began the process of packing. It brought painful memories of us leaving San Diego, but I powered through it.

We were blessed by family to help us move. Daelene and her husband, my son and family, Joe, Jr., Emma, Anthony, Marie, and Nicole, Jasper and Juliet, and a dear friend, whom I now call sister, Akoni, and her husband Tané all joined us to accomplish this giant task.

Akoni is the grandmother of Jasper and Juliet's little sister, Hokulani, by their father, Keith. Akoni, like me, is raising her granddaughter. Hokulani wanted to know her brother and sister, so Akoni reached out to me. Jasper, Juliet, and I met up with them when she was three. Since that day Akoni and my bond has grown to that of sisters.

Our new rental was larger than our first. I had enough space in my bedroom to establish an office—a perfect place for writing which I never made time for. It had an open bedroom for the children to use as a game room. It had a front porch I always dreamed of but forgot it the minute I walked into the house. It was a beautiful home, but I kept waiting for the other shoe to drop.

We lived there for the first year, and in November they upped our rent to almost breaking point. I had to renew the lease as we weren't prepared to do anything else. Funds would be tight for a while. Anxiety filled me, and worry gnawed at me about the next lease period. I couldn't be caught off guard for a second time, and I knew in my gut they would increase the rent again. I knew we had to move because we couldn't afford living there anymore. We established a pattern of moving every two years, but it had to stop because the rent was increasing in our area.

We had to act, but I didn't know what that looked like.

CHAPTER 9

RESTRICT YOUR PROGRESS

Overcome your own worst enemy. Defeat the imposter inside. Become a Phoenix Rising.

The brain is powerful. As you examine the different parts, you'll find some are more powerful than others.

The Neurosurgery Department of UPMC, University of Pittsburgh Medical Center, states, "The limbic system is a set of brain structures containing the pleasure center [and emotional life, i.e. emotion (including fear), behavior, and motivation] while the prefrontal cortex controls planning and decision making. The prefrontal cortex is less developed and thus weaker …"[2]

There is a physiological response in your body when you live in fear and stress. You are living in your limbic system which was the first part of the brain formed in prehistoric man. You are operating in flight or fight mode constantly. There is no moving up into your prefrontal cortex where planning, decision making, and creativity reside.

You are literally putting one foot in front of the other in rote action. These are behaviors you've honed and require no thought. It takes effort to move and stay in your prefrontal cortex. You must retrain your brain to do so.

• • •

I was my own worst enemy when I moved to San Diego.

Fear overtook me, and *fight or flight* was my environment. I worried about the children—who would watch them on the weekend if I didn't have a Monday through Friday job? Massage therapist positions always worked on Saturdays. Would I earn enough to support us? Fear compelled me to seek a *traditional job* with a Monday-Friday schedule, and I found one.

I descended into the rote action of the limbic system. We woke, I took them to school, I went to work, I picked them up from football and cheerleading practice, we had dinner, and went to bed. And it all began again the next day. The weekends were for household chores, laundry, occasional outings to the beach, spending time with Mike and sometimes with my YaYa's.

My truth, my objective of being of service to others, was abandoned when I made the move to San Diego. The whole reason I became a massage therapist was to have a flexible schedule so I could write and that was tossed aside. I became an imposter in my own life. Again.

Why would I allow myself to become an imposter when I worked so hard to establish my authenticity? It was my self-limiting beliefs of not being good enough.

I moved my fears up to Washington with me. I started looking for that elusive full-time job that would give benefits to carry me through to my retirement age of 67. I would be tied to a desk for over a decade, but it would be safe. However, Creator had different plans for me. An office job was not a choice for me anymore. If I had understood this, life would have been more bearable.

Being accepted back into the fold of massage therapy was the first right decision I made upon returning. There is an art to massage. There is a connection to Creator and energy flow with the massage therapist as a conduit to the patient. There are skilled massage techniques employed in the therapist/patient partnership. This is who I am.

Even with this connection to Creator, I was still caught up in survival mode with my grandkids and with the tension and stress of everyday living. I reacted to their behavior instead of absorbing and listening with my heart.

Jasper, Juliet, and I continued in this merry go round fashion; routine movement but not really going anywhere until the end of December 2017. A long three years of being my own worst enemy.

What was the impetus for my 'aha' moment? Perhaps it was the influx of messages from influencers the likes of Deepak Chopra or Oprah. Maybe it was my daily meditation, my opening up to Creator during Sunday service, and truly participating as a member of the church. Perhaps it was surrounding myself with like-minded people whose energy combined and magnified my own. I wish I could pinpoint it, but nonetheless, I am glad for it. All I know is I went from survival mode, also known as my limbic system, to slowly peeling back my imposter layers, my insecurities, my restrictions to my authentic self/my inner child to utilize my prefrontal cortex in the manifestation of my intentions.

We were facing a rent increase we couldn't afford. This was approximately November 2017, and my lease would be renewed in February 2018.

I shared my dilemma with a friend who happened to be a real estate agent. She worked in a unique partnership with a lender and a broker. Everything sounded ideal so I hired her early November 2017.

I provided all my documents to the lender within several days. Then I waited. For weeks. There was a snag with their process, and we were stalled. They couldn't give me a firm answer to the amount we qualified for, so my agent's hands were tied. I could hear time ticking away. In response, I threw away part of my savings and extended my lease by one month.

Frustration and concern were overflowing—we needed to find a house by the end of March, or I'd be paying more than we had. Something had to be done—the lender wasn't moving forward. I put my trust in the power of the Divine and utilized one of Creator's tools: manifesting.

There are three steps leading up to manifestation. The first is setting the intention. To set an intention is to identify events or things you want to happen in your life, such as my move to San Diego.

The second step is focused meditation. You see in your mind's eye successful completion of your intention. During my focused meditation, I saw my move to San Diego: the pack out, the drive, and living in an apartment.

The third step is to work your intentions. You need an action plan for each one. Brainstorm or meditate on what steps you need to follow, and Creator will give you the information you need. This can be done in an instant or could take place over time. It will always be about connecting the dots to manifest it in your life.

I knew I could manifest my house because I manifested the move to San Diego. However, harsh lessons were learned which I needed to avoid. I needed help and Creator stepped in. A Vision Board class was held at my church on New Year's Eve 2017. The Vision Board would provide the clarity and focus I needed.

For those unfamiliar with the concept of a Vision Board, it's a collage of images and words representing what you want in your life. The middle of my board reflected what I wanted most to manifest. The bottom center was my need to have our house.

My house intention was specific. It had to be in in the same school zone as the kids were attending. They didn't need any further disruption in their lives. The house cost must fit our budget, have four bedrooms, and a bathtub in the master bath.

My writing intention was at the top. I realized clarity was missing as I had not published a book before. My collage was created with my novel in mind. The main picture was of the locale of my fictional story, and the remaining pictures reflected what I believed was the route an author would take.

I worked on my Vision Board. I mounted it where I would see it before I went to bed at night and when I woke in the morning. Prior to sleep, I meditated on it for two minutes, and when I woke, I did the same. The house purchase was crucial, so I completed an extra 10-minute meditation every night.

Working my Vision Board in this manner was important, but it wasn't the end of the process. I opened myself to Creator to receive my action plan, and the steps were provided. I left my writing intention alone since we would move in two months.

The Wells Fargo logo first appeared in my mind, then I saw it everywhere. This was the first item in my action plan. I reached out to them for help, and their Home Mortgage Consultant, Theresa, was invaluable in the help she gave me. I was approved for a loan almost immediately and house hunting began.

Our agent found a one-story with green eaves and even greener grass in the right location, but we found it too late. We were in a seller's market, and our offer was the fourth one submitted. Our agent advocated for us, but our offer wasn't selected. We were hunting again.

Two days later, the kids and I joined our agent to look at another one-story with three bedrooms. The walls were closing in on me the minute we walked in. We wandered into the master bedroom, then the master bath. It only had a shower. This was a no-go for me, and the children agreed for their own reasons.

Jasper was on Zillow before we walked out the door. He found a two-story house in the right area, for the right price, and it had been listed an hour prior. The agent did her magic so when we arrived, we were able to view the house.

The house beamed like sunshine with its yellow siding. The front porch ran the length of the house—one of my secret desires. The children's bedrooms were upstairs along with the *loft* (the fourth bedroom), and the master bathroom had a bathtub. All my needs were met to include the location and the price. We put an offer in on January 19th, and they accepted it the next day.

Wells Fargo was meant to be our lender. A special loan/grant program partnered with Wells Fargo for applicants such as me. It would expire at the end of 2018, and we were fortunate to obtain it. If we had gone with a different lender, the special program wouldn't exist. The customer service Theresa provided went well beyond what the other lender offered. She and I texted beyond her work hours, even up to 10 p.m. and on weekends. She was much more than a home mortgage consultant, and I would recommend her to anyone.

We closed at the end of February and received our keys on March 3rd. Our agent, the children, and I walked through our house enjoying all that it represented. We wouldn't move every two years, and we had financial and emotional stability. I breathed out a relieved and contented sigh.

We closed the house to leave. On the other side of my dream porch was a six-foot-high bush. I walked toward it and realized I was looking at rose hips. Creator blessed our house with my favorite flowering plant—we had three rose bushes in our front garden.

From the Vision Board inception to finding our house was approximately 19 days.

On my Vision Board, I created my writing intention with as much clarity as I knew. I added pictures and phrases to encourage writing and a picture which represented the setting of my novel. I didn't work on my writing intention until the end of May. I was busy with the move and getting settled, of working, and raising teenagers.

In meditation, I asked for guidance regarding my writing intention. I asked to be more aware of opportunities that surrounded me, and for assistance in the development of my action plan.

Social media platform popped in my head. *Blogging* appeared next. Being open to Creator's guidance kept the messages coming in quickly, but I hit my first self-limiting belief, or so I thought. I knew how to blog, but I didn't know how to do it well.

I did a google search and found a blogging course titled Intentional Blog. The synchronicity of the course title blew me away. Setting and working intentions are part of my Intentional Living Toolbelt. This was the course for me.

My Intentional Living Toolbelt is a visualization of all the steps listed in the last part of this book; it's how I own my mirror. The Intentional Living Toolbelt will function the same for you as it does for me. It will hold all our tools, skills, and techniques we'll use in living an intentional life. After my experience in San Diego, I will never be without my Intentional Living Toolbelt.

I signed up for the blogging course and began the work. Creator seemed to be fixated on social media platforms as it was discussed in one of the modules. I already had Facebook and Instagram, and the logical part of my brain said these two platforms were enough. But I knew I had to explore Twitter, so I signed up. My second follow after Stephen King was the blogging course creator, James.

James announced he was attending the Influence and Impact Summit, a conference put together by a skilled marketer. The list of speakers was intriguing. They included publishers, authors, web designers, marketers, and of course James. I learned so many different aspects of the business side of writing.

On day two or three, a dynamic speaker, Kary Oberbrunner, took the stage. He shared his business, Author Academy Elite (AAE) and his passion for serving others.

AAE offers one-stop training and support in a unique setting—a Facebook group called Igniting Souls and the AAE website. Once a year this dynamic team holds an annual conference for the Igniting Souls tribe. We meet and learn more from these amazing people.

Kary and his team are AAE. They take you from book concept through marketing to collaborative publishing in 18 months or sooner. AAE offered all the Summit was offering plus five days of coaching calls each week covering writing, editing, author and business questions for 18 months. This is 390 coaching calls during the life of the program.

Their calls were true support and coaching. Each coach stayed on the call until all students had been served, their questions answered, confidence built back up, and successes recognized. Sometimes this could take over two hours per call.

I was led to Author Academy Elite. Creator knew my writing path and shared the steps with me. If I had missed one step, the blogging course, following James on Twitter, listening in on the Summit conference, or taking the leap of faith with Kary's team, you wouldn't be reading this book today. Within a year from starting with AAE, I published my first book. This has been my dream for the last 36 years.

The next part of this book will show how I found my authentic self and purpose, to serve, and to maintain my authenticity. You, too, can become a Phoenix Rising—flying up from the ashes of your former self, and re-emerging anew clothed in your purpose and identity.

PART FOUR

Own the Mirror!

INTRODUCTION TO PART FOUR

OWN THE MIRROR!

"Do the one thing you think you cannot do.
Fail at it. Try again. Do better the second time.
The only people who never tumble are those who
never mount the high wire.
This is your moment.
Own it."

-Oprah Winfrey

We've traveled many generations and covered the surface of my past. The transitions from childhood sexual abuse, keeping secrets, wearing labels, and trying to find balance were challenging.

Now, I'm a single grandma raising two teenage grandchildren, being a mom a second time around; I'm an elder in a society with changing expectations. This has brought a different set of challenges which I'm adapting to every day.

We've processed grief and loss along the way, also. The loss during divorce, even though it was my choice, takes its toll. The loss of one child to drugs. The loss of the opportunity to find myself due to care-taking my mother and grandchildren. The loss of self when one feels cut off from Creator.

Three aspects of loss I've not experienced yet, but have been shared with me, are the loss of self during retirement, an illness, and becoming an empty nester. These are all major life changes you don't really prepare for. You're taking action, making decisions right up to the day these events occur. Then, suddenly, you're right in the middle of the unknown. You're struggling with no direction.

If what I've shared so far makes you say, *I've felt that before,* I encourage you to use the discussion points in Appendix I. Document the changes you may have experienced in your life and find your authentic self.

In Part 4, I outlined the steps I used to find my authentic self. These steps will be effective for you no matter why you're looking for your identity or purpose if you do the work.

The Creator provided these 13 steps for Intentional Living. The key is to establish your authentic self and purpose, hold on to it, and work to keep it. We are all human and will fall backward from time to time. That's okay, and you need to forgive yourself.

Here's to owning your mirror!

• • •

Part Four is shaped by three chapters which contain the 13 steps to Intentional Living. These steps should be added to your Intentional Living Toolbelt to be accessed whenever you find yourself sliding back into self-limiting habits.

Chapter 10, Develop Your Path, outlines eight steps to overcome the imposter within and discover who you truly are.

Chapter 11, Shape Your Environment, gives three steps to create your inner world.

Chapter 12, Embody Your Change, presents two steps to implement habits to maintain your authentic self.

CHAPTER 10
DEVELOP YOUR PATH

This chapter outlines eight steps to overcome the imposter within and discover who you truly are.

Step 1 - Free Your Authentic Self

Your authentic self is the core of who you are, your identity. In most cases, one's authentic self has been repressed by life events. In order to free yourself, you must peel back the layers. There are a number of steps in doing this. Before you begin, please seek counseling when you need it. Remember, seeking counseling or a therapist when you're sad, overwhelmed or simply feeling *off* should be as routine as seeking a doctor when you feel sick.

Loving yourself without reservation is the first step. Do you truly love yourself? Or do you carry intentional or unintentional self-limiting beliefs which block your view of your authentic self?

A self-limiting belief is the doubt or fear you carry. Some are intentional. Some examples are keeping family secrets to minimize perceived shame such as mental illness, unlawful behavior, substance abuse. Or the common *who do I think I am*? i.e. "I'm not knowledgeable or have the authority to speak on a topic or apply for higher level positions." It can be advice from your spouse or loved one as they try to protect you from a potential perceived hurt when in actuality, they're uncomfortable with the steps you're taking in uncovering your identity.

Unintentional self-limiting beliefs are ones you're born into. They can range from the experiences your parents had as children and are now visited upon you, such as creating the definition of 'wife/husband' or 'mother/father'. They can be your environment; living in a dangerous neighborhood or negativity found in the school system. It can be your lack of nurturing, for example, neglect, mental or verbal abuse, or physical or sexual abuse.

After examining your life, do you have self-limiting beliefs? What are you going to do with them? Do you need help processing them? Find a therapist to walk with you as you work through them. There is no shame in this. It demonstrates your strength when you ask for help.

Second, you'll need to peel off each layer, each hurt, and forgive. I know this is difficult, but it is necessary to move forward in your life.

I had to do it and am still doing it specifically for the sexual abuse that I experienced. I was hurting for my inner child. I've cried for the loss of innocence. I was angry it happened and angry that I felt I couldn't tell anyone. I'm comfort eating as of this writing (meaning I'm eating whether I'm hungry or not) to fill the void this act has created in me. I have forgiven because holding onto anger only keeps me rooted in the past. I still have work to do, but I am moving forward with the help of a therapist.

Peel off each tie that binds you and forgive. This could be a long process, but it is so important. My best practice is using a mental and physical activity to transfer the hurt, anger, and forgiveness into an inanimate object. Once transferred, the object is removed from my home.

Since I have an affinity with rocks, I chose one for this purpose. Through meditation, I transfer all the emotions into my special rock. I take the rock and bury it in the front garden to give the energy back to Mother Earth.

An alternative is to add each object to your altar for continued blessings. If you have a collection, you can bury them all at once or set up a display in your garden.

Some people write a letter to the person or situation which caused the self-limiting belief. When done, they burn it or destroy it. The choice is yours in how you process and dispose of it.

There are a variety of ways to process each trauma. What will you choose?

Third, you need to own your reaction to the event. This means you take full responsibility for your response to the event or take part ownership in it. I take half of the responsibility for the ending of my marriage. Communication was not our strength, but I could've have tried harder to talk to my ex. I own my response to my sexual abuse. As an adult, not the child I was. It happened, and there is nothing I can do now to change it. My choice is to live constrained by the action, or I can come to terms with it and move forward. I choose to move forward to remove the anchors it has attached to my life.

There are three things you're in control of: how you think, what you visualize, and your response.

You can respond without taking responsibility with thoughts like "It's not my fault I don't have money." "I don't like the way my boss is treating me." "I don't have time to work out." "I don't have time to eat healthy food."

What did you spend your paycheck on? Did you pay bills? Are you living in a place you can't afford? Did you only spend your extra money? If you spent your money wisely, maybe it's time to find a higher paying job or career. This may mean you go back to school. Is it daunting to face this choice? Of course, it is. But break it into bite size chunks by planning, and then execute the plan. If you didn't spend your money wisely, create and stick to a budget.

"I don't have time to work out." Or "I'm too tired after my workday to exercise." Have you mapped out your day to find your free time? I was this person saying both: I don't have time to work out, and I'm too tired to exercise.

Exercising at the end of my work day didn't happen—I was too tired after massaging, and I didn't want to get up any earlier than 6 a.m. This was my normal wake up when the kids were in school. I felt justified in not exercising.

However, our bodies are meant for movement and after reflection, I mapped out my day to find when I could exercise. Guess where I found it? I found it at 5 a.m. I sat and looked at my day and tried to find another time to no avail. It was 5 a.m. No getting around it. Cycling on my stationary bike every day at 5 a.m. is part of who I am now. It throws off my day if I can't fit it in. Another positive is cycling is a non-cognitive activity which allows one to do other things.

Since cycling doesn't require attention I'm able to meditate, watch educational videos, or listen to podcasts without conflict. Thinking outside the box, even a little, makes our days more manageable.

I know I make this sound easy, but that's far from the case. It takes work to change your self-limiting beliefs, to change your world view, to assert yourself, and stay strong in your authentic self. It takes courage to face possible failure (life lessons), or confrontation, disapproval, or the skepticism of others.

Your hard work and perseverance will be worth it as you journey in freeing your authentic self.

Step 2 - Brainstorm Your Purpose

You've identified most of the invisible chains holding your inner child down and found a way to work them. You have established a way to heal either on your own or with the help of a therapist.

Now what? What should your next step be?

It's time to find your purpose. Now is the time to figure out what your interests, talents, and points of service are. You may have already figured this out, but with the shackles removed from your inner child, things may look different, or you don't feel the same about them anymore.

Maybe you've experienced a major life event which brings you to this point. It could be divorce, retirement, serious illness, empty nester, loss of a loved one, or loss of a job.

You've counted the days until your retirement, and you're the star of the party. You visit with all the people who've come to wish you well. As the day ends, everyone says goodbye and now you're home alone or with your significant other. What now?

Or your last child leaves the nest. They are living life on their own, and you've no one to care for or help with their life choices. You've dedicated yourself as *mother/father* without establishing who you are, or what your purpose is.

A new day dawns and you're not busy. You have time to reflect on you, and it makes you uncomfortable. You now have the freedom to do whatever you want, but you don't know what to do or where to start. Or, as in my case, I was devasted with the loss of the children even though it was for three weeks. I cried at night, feeling lost, and without purpose.

A serious or life-threatening illness will make you step back and take stock of where you are. Each moment is precious, and it's important to make the most of your time. Yet, you're apprehensive about making a decision for fear you won't be able to complete it.

In all the examples I gave you, you will experience loss. Loss of your marriage even if you were the one to initiate it because there were good times, loss of your mother or father—or in my case loss of both of my parents, loss of your sense of purpose in retirement, loss of self when unemployed and it's difficult to find a job, or loss of your health.

This is the time to grieve for what was lost; honor it, give it it's due in emotion and holding space for it. How much time you should take is ultimately your decision, but it's easy to get lost in the grieving process and forget your purpose.

Now is the time to re-evaluate your purpose or decide on one that truly resonates with you.

How do you begin? One way is to Map your interests.

• • •

Part I.

What do you feel are your limitations?

What are your strengths?

Do you have an underlying goal you want to accomplish?

Part II.
Do you want to enhance or share what is in your comfort zone? Or do you want to try something new?
Let's explore some areas or you can add to the list.

Do you want to work with?

- Animals
- Humane Society, Fostering
- Children/Teens
    - Mentors, Coaches, GS/BS Leaders, Volunteer in Schools
- Elderly
    - Offer classes in senior centers in wherever your talents lie, etc.
    - Volunteer in Assisted Living/Nursing Homes
- Personal Growth:
    - Pursue higher education resulting in a certification or degree
    - Adult classes in areas which pique your interest

Your Thoughts: Are there other areas not covered above you wish to explore?

Or do you want to take your pain point and use it to serve others? My personal pain point was to overcome my imposter inside and to discover who I truly was. My intention is to help others not experience decades of following society's expectation of defining self, for people to declare who they truly are, and live an authentic life.

What is your pain point, and what can you do with it?

Step 3 - Stay Strong

You may have lived an imposter existence for a while now. I actively lived one from when I was 18 to 57. Your family and friends see you as you portrayed yourself over the years. Attempting to change will cause some discomfort, much like an oyster dealing with a grain of sand.

But you are making changes in your life. Some changes may be small and accepted readily. Or the changes may be significant, and cause discomfort with your family. Typically, the reason for their displeasure is you're interrupting their worldview, i.e. their view of themselves and their view of you.

Be prepared for the full gamut of reactions from skepticism, confrontation, disbelief, disapproval, support, and others which may be specific to you. Your partner/ loved ones may not be aware of your despondency so your changes might come as a shock, and they may react harshly.

If you want to preserve your relationship(s), it's your responsibility to communicate and explain why you're making these changes. It's important you know why you're making them and can share them clearly and succinctly.

Your next step is to write out, videotape, or audio tape (self-talk), your change, your reasons why, and how you're taking ownership of the change.

For example, "I'm writing a book about how my life was impacted by societal expectations, cultural beliefs, and sexual abuse." I want to write my book to help other people overcome the imposter inside, define their identities, and live their authentic life.

• • •

What is/are your change(s)?

What is/are your reason(s)?

What is your calm response to their reaction?

Your goal is to help them smooth over their discomfort like the oyster making a pearl, to remain calm even though it feels as if they're attacking you personally, and to stay strong in becoming your authentic self.

Remember to bolster yourself through prayer, meditation, and/or whatever connections you have in your belief system. Creator wants you to be your authentic self and serve in whatever capacity this may be.

Step 4 - Ho'oponopono

Ho'oponopono is a Hawaiian practice of forgiveness.

I was introduced to Ho'oponopono by a Kahuna at a retreat in a Hawaiian massage school many years ago. The Kahuna explained Ho'oponopono means to *make right more right.*

All of us gathered together and he opened the session with pule (prayer) and Ha (breath work - 30 deep, vocal breaths) before we shared what was troubling us.

In the book, *Wise Secrets of Aloha: Learn and Live the Sacred Art of Lomilomi,* "The Ha Breath is a powerful healing tool." (P. 65) "The real conduit of healing, the core, is in using breath as a medicine. Breathwork is primarily grace receiving gratitude." (P. 63) "Breath—deep, powerful breath beginning in the diaphragm, at the solar plexus, the space between the lungs and stomach—where the power to heal comes through." (P. 64) Seventy percent of toxins are released with this forceful breathwork.

Each of us was honored by the other members of the circle as we shared what was troubling our inner selves. We said the four statements to ourselves: 'I'm sorry. Please forgive me. Thank you. I love you'. We ended the circle with pule and moved onto the Lomilomi (Hawaiian massage) session to imbed the healing we experienced into our bodies.

Ho'oponopono evolved as a means of resolving conflicts in families which could be the reason for illness. According to *Nā Mo'olelo Lomilomi, The Traditions of Hawaiian Massage and Healing,* "Families used ho'oponopono to reconcile their differences and to forgive one another so they could resolve the underlying causes of illness." (P. 39) An elder of the family would facilitate the gathering and encourage other members to talk of their hurts. The elder would open and close the session with pule and the intent that the issue would be resolved at this point.

"Ho'oponopono is also used to heal relationships between people, nature, and Ke Akua (God). Ho'oponopono is variously translated as 'setting to right,' 'forgiveness,' 'reconciliation,' or 'family counseling." (P. 47)

Ho'oponopono has been widely accepted and used outside of its Hawaiian traditions and origins. The basis of its effectiveness is in the four statements mentioned above directed at yourself, your family, or your ancestors You say them when you feel negative emotions, i.e. anger, shame, or hurt. You take ownership of the unease and forgive your reaction to the event.

"I'm sorry." For having these perceptions or beliefs of what people have done to you.

"Please forgive me." For being upset by what is going on, for my lack of compassion, for my negative beliefs.

"Thank you." For removing the negative beliefs, for making me one again.

"I love you." For bringing me back in sync with my purpose, for loving me unconditionally.

Utilization of the Ho'oponopono mantra, the four statements, is recommended to be done each time you have negative feelings or unease, or at least daily. It is especially recommended when you are working *Step 1 - Free Your Authentic Self.*

Step 5 - Establish Your Beliefs

Deep down inside, everyone has self-doubt and/or fear. We can't avoid it. It could stem from our parents attempting to protect our psyche when we were children. Or maybe we experienced traumatic events while young. However it was developed, we have one or more.

This self-doubt or fear is self-limiting beliefs as described in *Step 1 - Free Your Authentic Self.* We peel them off as in pulling leaves off an artichoke. Eventually, we reach the heart of the artichoke, which represents our inner child or authentic self.

Now that you're there, what's next?

It's time to establish your empowered belief system.

How does one do this?

Make a list of the things you peeled off in *Step 1 - Free Your Authentic Self.*

Here are some examples of your inner self-talk:

- "A man should provide for you. Whatever job the wife held was to support the family while the real breadwinner was the husband."
    - You believe you don't have any talents of your own. You're the supporting actor.

  (Society has pinned this belief on many of the baby-boomers whose dads went to work while moms stayed home to raise the children.)

- "Children are seen and not heard."
    - You believe you must be quiet in order to be loved.
- "You can't be a writer or other artistic endeavor because it's not a real job. You need to have a real job."

- You believe they don't have faith in you. Your dreams are of no consequence.

So now take these beliefs and turn it around into something positive and turn them into a mantra.

- You are worthy and capable of taking care of yourself. You have knowledge, skills, and abilities an employer will value.
  - **Mantra**: I am an asset to my employer.
- You are an equal and valuable partner in your marriage.
  - **Mantra**: I am an equal partner in my marriage.
- Your innate talents lie in many areas. All things take practice to develop an accomplished skill set.
  - **Mantra**: My talents are varied and valued.
- You are loved for who you are in whatever package you come in.
  - **Mantra**: I am beautiful and loved.
- You are gifted and talented. Follow your dreams—they're your dreams and don't require approval from anyone else. If you don't make a wholehearted attempt at achieving them, it will affect you at different times of your life.
  - **Mantra**: I am working and living my dream.
  - **Mantra:** I am gifted and talented.

Turn all the self-limiting beliefs you identified into positives and develop your mantras. Buy or make a calendar and post it in your bathroom. Look in the mirror and state one to two mantras every day for 90 days. Make a red *X* on each day you state your mantras. Once you hit 90 days you're done with that set. It's time to move onto the next set. If you miss a day of saying your mantras, you must start your 90 days all over again.

By saying them for 90 days without fail, you're taking these thoughts and turning them into beliefs by repeating them. The more you believe, the more they will come true.

Step 6 - Find Your Tribe

A tribe is your group of people who are moving in the same direction as you and will support you as you support them. They can be your family, friends, business colleagues, or spiritual family.

The tribe surrounding you now was formed before you discovered your authentic self. They may not understand your transition. If these are relationships you value, then you need to salvage them if you can. Reference *Step 3 — Stay Strong.*

Not all of them will want to be part of your life so be prepared to let them go. It's to be expected, and you will grieve. Grieving is part of the process of allowing your authentic self to be birthed.

The people who remain in your reflection are those you began this journey with. They are a rich pool of love and support but may contain unknowns because like you, they are works in progress. What they see now is comfortable for them as they love you. As you continue to grow, they may become uncomfortable with your changes and may share their discontent with you. Be ready for this.

In *Step 3 - Stay Strong*, you need to be confident in your choices and reasons why you've adjusted your path. You don't need to explain yourself, but to ease your family and friends discomfort it's important to do so. Keep in mind you're making them look at their life through a magnifying glass; it's a natural response to your changes.

Share how meaningful it is to you to follow your path. Given time to process, your friends and family may come to understand and embrace you. If they understand, they'll become your tribe and stand with you. Show them your enthusiasm for your authentic self. If they don't understand, say goodbye for now. With reflection, they may yet embrace you, but don't wait for them.

It's important to continue to build your tribe with like-minded people as you pursue your purpose. Network with your tribe in seeking knowledge they may have in this area. If you've discovered your purpose is to write a book, you'll associate with other writers through different writing venues. If through peeling back the layers you've discovered you're interested in a certain belief system, i.e. spirituality, Christianity, Buddhism, or another religion, you'll find like-minded people as you explore their places of worship or other venues as you do your research. If you want to change occupations, the same applies as you find others in that line of work.

Usually, an area of interest will have a group of people gathering to share in experiences, knowledge, and community. You'll find it's true for amateur rocket builders, racquetball enthusiasts, massage therapists, car clubs, reiki practitioners, teachers, entrepreneurs, and the list continues. The beauty of internet search engines like Google, Bing, and others make finding other like-minded people easy.

These new tribe members will prop you up when you feel yourself flagging in face of possible disapproving reactions and your own negative self-talk. And you may be filling a need within their lives. They will be filling up your tribe, and you will be filling up theirs.

Congratulations, you're building your tribe.

Step 7 - Clear Your Clutter

Have you ever walked into a store and been overwhelmed by the sheer amount of merchandise they offer? A long-awaited craft store was coming to my town. They had advertised for months and the hype won me over. Brimming with excitement I skipped in to see all the goods they had. I skidded to a stop—I was dazed.

The store was filled with *STUFF!* In front of me were waist high racks of bric-a-brac sorted in colors. To the right was the floral department—single stemmed foliage and flowers loomed overshadowing the six to ten-inch potted plants. To the left were shelves and shelves of goods, but it all melded together into puddles of browns, greens, neutrals, metals that assaulted my eyes and tried to penetrate my brain. There were so many things to look at it, and I hadn't made it to the center of the store yet. It was overwhelming to take it all in. I had to leave to calm my senses.

As I sat in my car, I knew I had to reframe my mind before going back in. I had to look at each section for what it offered. Stepping back into the store I was armed with my strategy. I looked at the areas systematically and figured out their layout. I took the time to become familiar with their product groupings, and what they had to offer. I was there for specific items, so it became easier to track them down.

I acted on my feelings in this situation of being overwhelmed and came to peace with my emotions. I *self-talked*, produced an action plan, and implemented it. I realize this was low on the scale of stressors, but it was best to have a small event to work through.

I was given an opportunity to practice gaining control over an overwhelming situation. The more we practice the more adept we become with multiple stressors and/or high-tension situations.

All of us have clutter—physical and mental clutter which affects us. I have a garage filled with furniture, boxes from my ex-husband, lawn and garden equipment—it's become my *fling it room.* My mental clutter covers raising my teenage grandchildren, through my massage therapy career, household responsibilities, and launching my entrepreneurial career. My responsibilities include coordinating the children's health care, car care, house care, work requirements, and the myriad of steps in publishing, marketing, and being impactful with my book.

Now, how about you? What clutter are you confronted with? Are there physical ones such as?

- Dishes in the sink because you didn't take care of it the night before.
- Mail piled on your desk from the past week.
- Mounds of laundry.
- Weeds overtaking your lawn and garden.
- Your day job is sucking all your energy from you, and you can't motivate yourself to touch anything?

What about mental clutter?

- You have a list of household tasks to complete.
- The doctor appointments you need to schedule.
- Arrange care for your grandkids while you go out of town.
- Continuing education for your career.

- o Holiday and birthday gifts which need to be bought.
- o Bills that need to be paid.

The list seems never-ending.

We all have many responsibilities on our shoulders. How do we manage our tasks if we can't get ourselves organized? Add from a single parent perspective? Or from a breadwinner perspective when you're holding down a 9-5 job and starting up your own business? Or from this same perspective and your spouse isn't shouldering their share of the load? How do we balance it, and be successful?

The first step, I believe, is cleaning out the clutter.

How do we know what clutter we have?

Take an inventory of all the areas you're responsible for, making a list of things to take care of.

- o Household tasks.
- o Chores.
- o Family tasks.
- o Personal tasks.
- o Work tasks.

I'd suggest making lists that you can check off when you're done. You may need that instant gratification to continue the forward momentum. I personally need to check an item off my list to have a sense of accomplishment. Making a list ensures I don't miss an important step, and I keep it all on my smart phone. The Notes iPhone application is my lifesaver and it's always at my fingertips. If electronic tools work for you, you can find them on your phone or tablet. If pen and paper/calendar feels right to you, there are many options you can find at stores like Walmart and Target or office supply stores.

Maintaining this type of organization in all areas of my life removes layers of responsibility from my shoulders so when unexpected high stress-events occur the routine daily tasks aren't forgotten. I really appreciated my lists when my car engine stopped in the fast lane of Interstate 5 and had to be towed, and when I was rear-ended on a different section of the highway seven months later.

We need to remember stress is also attached to positive changes in our lives, such as being promoted within your company, starting a new job, going back to school, becoming a caretaker for your grandchildren, and being recognized for your personal achievements.

Some lists may cover labor-intensive tasks, like chores. I recommend taking a weekend to complete the tasks you can get done.

- Clean out the garage.
- Make and install window screens.
- Make a garden.

Have you talked with your spouse/significant other? You can make it a family objective to have a Clear the Clutter Day, especially if the kids are young. Make it a game with a tangible reward. Establish a reward for yourself also, or maybe having time to work on your purpose is reward enough.

You've set up lists to remove clutter and stay organized for your routine responsibilities. Your next step is to allow time for completion of your personal intention, your purpose. How much time do you need to focus on it? What are the tasks? Do you have support from your family? These all play a factor in what you need to do. Remember to stay present in every task you undertake.

Figure out what your guidelines are for researching and/or working your purpose. Best practice is meditation when you're facing these types of questions or dilemmas. Receiving guidance from Creator through prayer, reflection/meditation, is crucial to your success.

If you're a strong manifestor like Oprah Winfrey, a vision board isn't necessary. Accountability for your goals is. You may have started with a vague intention but through following Creator's messages you will find your path has become more defined. You may need to course adjust and document it to stay in line with your purpose.

What is a vision board? A vision board is a common tool used to identify what you want to bring into your life. One identifies goals or intentions and pastes it onto a board. It's ok to flip forward to this step in the book to receive more definitive information on it (See *Step 11 — Establish Your Intentions.*).

Bottom line—it works!

Step 8 - Maintain Your Health

When I speak of health, I mean all aspects of your health; i.e. your personal trinity of mind, body, and spirit. It is important to stay at your healthiest in these areas as you need to be effective in your purpose. If you're ailing, you're not giving 100% to the areas you're responsible for. I suggest you take a good look at all of three of these areas to determine where you may need healing.

Physical Health

The most common one we look at is our physical health; specifically, we need to look at exercise, nutrition, sleep habits, and fluid intake. A healthy body is important to the balance of all aspects of your life.

How do you rate your overall health? Excellent, Good, Fair, or Poor? However you rate it I believe there's always room for improvement, even at Excellent.

Your body is made for movement. With the approval of your doctor, you should initiate a movement regimen if you haven't done so. Ideally, the exercises should increase your heart rate. Seek information from a reputable source about the recommended activity for your body type, age, and ability.

My mom showed me how inactivity affects the body. As she was getting older, she moved less and less. When she lived with me, she sat in her room watching TV and would only come out for meals. I tried to motivate her, but she always said it hurt her to move.

When she was released from the nursing home after shattering her hip, I helped her do her prescribed exercises by walking a circuit we had in the house. Most of the time she fought me, not wanting to walk. The distance was short, but it moved her muscles.

Professor Bryant Stamford, Chairman of the Department of Kinesiology and Integrative Physiology stated, "...when you don't use your muscles, you send a message that they are not important. In response, your body quits supporting your muscles with energy, which causes them to atrophy (shrink)."[3]

Unfortunately, when mom relocated to an assisted living facility and then to a nursing home, less importance was put on her walking/moving. I don't know if it was from a lack of adequate staffing at these facilities, or they complied with her wishes to remain in her room. Her quality of life suffered for it, and I believe, she sunk deeper into depression.

Like mother like daughter. After she passed away, I found myself sitting in my recliner instead of moving. My hips were painful, and it was easier to sit than to have any activity. It was a self-fulfilling prophecy. The less I moved the more it hurt when I finally had to move. It was easier to sit and read or watch TV than push myself to move.

When I reached 175 pounds on a 5'3" frame, I knew I had to do something instead of feeling sorry for myself. *Sorry* isn't the right emotion. I was disgusted with myself. I was punishing myself for not being all that I should have been for my mother. My excuse for not being there for mom could be raising my toddler grandchildren. However, it would be simply that: an excuse.

The extra weight increased the pain, so I sought medical help. My primary care physician (PCP) couldn't figure out what was wrong with me. He referred me to a rheumatologist who eventually diagnosed me with Post Strep Reactive Arthritis in my hips.

This diagnosis scared me. The rheumatologist explained I had strep throat at some point and either I didn't finish the antibiotics or didn't know I had strep and didn't seek medical attention. Strep migrates through the body if not taken care of by antibiotics, and can settle anywhere—in your brain, in your heart, in your lungs, or in my case my hips.

Long story short, she was wrong. I spent three long years of a five-year regimen on antibiotics for a condition I didn't have. If massage school hadn't enlightened me, I would've believed my rheumatologist. I would've taken another two years of antibiotics I didn't need.

I was angry my rheumatologist misdiagnosed me. I was angry I was ingesting an antibiotic I didn't need for three years. I didn't know what to do with this anger, so I buried it. Another layer of *life* I smothered my inner child with.

Creator put me in a position to quiz my physiology instructor about rheumatoid conditions. Armed with this knowledge, I went back to my PCP who referred me to another rheumatologist. The new doctor confirmed my suspicions. I did not have a rheumatoid condition other than fibromyalgia.

But what was wrong with me? My PCP referred me for an MRI on my left hip.

Upon this conclusive test, I was diagnosed with a torn left Gluteus Medius tendon; the section of the muscle which attaches to your femur (your leg bone). The cause of the tear was a too tight IT (Iliotibial) Band. This band runs from your hip to your knee.

The moral of my story is to listen to the messages Creator gives you. If I hadn't enrolled in the massage program, I wouldn't have had the opportunity to ask the physiology instructor about my erroneous diagnosis nor the importance of movement in the human body.

I knew I had to add some form of aerobic activity to my daily schedule. The only time available was in the morning. I hated, literally hated, the idea of getting up any earlier than 6 a.m., my normal rising time, to wake the children for school. My choice was to rise an hour earlier to achieve the 30 minutes of stationary cycling or complain about not having enough time to exercise. I changed my mindset to accept the earlier rise time knowing it was beneficial for my health. After three months of this routine, I feel great. I feel out of sync with myself if I miss a day, so I try to avoid missing my routine.

Where do you fall in this grouping? No movement except for daily activities including work? Some movement? Or are you on top of your exercise regimen? Wherever you are, remember to consult a doctor before starting a new exercise routine. I suggest hiring a personal trainer, if you're able, to ensure you're working your body correctly.

Your choice of foods, drink, and chemicals affect your body. There is a saying, *you are what you eat.* I believe it.

The kids and I have two black panthers named Freya and Pi. When we adopted our cats, they had coarse coats. I believe in feeding our animals quality food within our budget. Now their coats are silky and smooth which is a direct contrast to when they first came home with us. Seeing is believing for me.

I believe in eating a balanced diet based on my personal health, not what the current generic fads or recommendations are. My downfall is portion sizes. I struggle with second servings, as well.

It's so easy to eat poorly in our society. We're programmed to have a busy life of employment and/or pursuit of higher education, household care, maintenance of relationships, and perceived social obligations. Throw in any additional unexpected stressors, such as car troubles, being sick or depressed, a major issue with your home, children's social, emotional or academic difficulties, and the amount of time you have available to you is decreased. Now you need to fit in those pre-empted activities back into your schedule. And you still must eat! Ack! So you pull into a fast food restaurant, and/or take everyone out to a local restaurant.

Most restaurants design their menus to encourage patrons to visit repeatedly. We shouldn't blame them; this is their livelihood. We, however, become addicted to their foods because we like to eat foods high in carbohydrates and sugars.

I do the same thing, hit up a fast food place, when I'm not on the top of my game. Being on the top of my game means I plan out my meals, grocery shop on my designated day, and include meal prep to that day's routine. For example, today my shift begins at 10.30 a.m., and I'll be home by 7 p.m. I have a pork roast slowly cooking in my crock pot to become kālua pig, a Hawaiian dish my grandchildren and I love. Add rice (regular for the children and riced cauliflower for me) and cabbage and you have dinner and hopefully leftovers.

Successful management of your nutrition is to be proactive rather than reactive. Add meal planning and grocery shopping to your calendar every week or whatever frequency you choose. Be in control of what you put into your body. I know this sounds simplistic, but putting this into a routine requires thought, energy, and action. I can get side-tracked by my life and if I'm not prepared, I'll stumble and fall back on the fast food joint down the road.

Sleep is so important, the National Heart, Blood and Lung Institute published an article on it. "Sleep plays a vital role in good health and well-being throughout your life. Getting enough quality sleep at the right times can help protect your mental health, physical health, quality of life, and safety.

The way you feel while you're awake depends in part on what happens while you're sleeping. During sleep, your body is working to support healthy brain function and maintain your physical health. In children and teens, sleep also helps support growth and development.

The damage from sleep deficiency can occur in an instant (such as a car crash), or it can harm you over time. For example, ongoing sleep deficiency can raise your risk for some chronic health problems [i.e. obesity, high blood pressure, and others]. It also can affect how well you think, react, work, learn, and get along with others."[4]

What are your sleep habits? Are you getting the right amount of sleep a night? According to the National Sleep Foundation, teens 14-17 years old are recommended 8-10 hours, adults 18-64 years old are recommended 7-9 hours of sleep per night, and adults 65 and older are recommended 7-8 hours of sleep. Also, the quality of your sleep is equally as important. Are you getting quality sleep?

For years I thought I had been. I sleep alone, even during my married years since my ex-husband was gone a lot, so I really didn't have anyone to monitor my sleeping habits. I've been told I don't snore and in fact, it's hard to see if I'm breathing, but my legs do the *river dance* while I'm asleep. I didn't connect my daily tiredness and dozing off in my recliner to a sleep disorder so when Daelene suggested I talk to my PCP about her results and my symptoms it made sense. He referred me to a sleep doctor, and I was diagnosed with sleep apnea and restless leg syndrome.

Are you monitoring your water intake? Are you consuming enough water for the different situations you encounter such as your environment, exercising, pregnancy, or are you sick? I used the word *consuming* mindfully because we not only drink water, but we ingest it as well through foods high in water content.

The MAYO clinic tells us the health benefits of water:

Water is your body's principal chemical component and makes up about 60 percent of your body weight. Your body depends on water to survive.

Every cell, tissue, and organ in your body needs water to work properly. For example, water:

- Gets rid of wastes through urination, perspiration and bowel movements
- Keeps your temperature normal
- Lubricates and cushions joints
- Protects sensitive tissues

Lack of water can lead to dehydration—a condition that occurs when you don't have enough water in your body to carry out normal functions. Even mild dehydration can drain your energy and make you tired."[5]

The amount of water you need is specific to you. However, the common rule of thumb is eight glasses of water per day or drink when you feel thirsty. Check with your doctor or nutritionist for the right amount for you.

Next, we'll look at your daily routines. Is your work schedule Monday-Friday with set hours of work? Or are you working varied days/hours during the week and possibly a weekend day or two? What are you doing on your days off?

What are you doing during your day? Are you sitting at a desk? Are you moving your body? How are you holding your body while you're doing your daily activities? Are you aware of your posture? Are you hunched in front of a computer? Are you standing all day?

Why am I asking about this? How you hold yourself influences how you think. If you've worked in the customer service industry, I'm sure you've heard *answer the phone with a smile no matter what you're feeling inside.* A smile will automatically put a positive tone in your voice. This holds true for your posture. If you're slumped over a desk, your mind will follow suit with feelings of tiredness, lack of energy, lack of motivation.

From a massage therapist perspective, how you hold your body while you're working could lead to repetitive stress injuries to muscles, tendons, nerves, and ligaments, i.e. carpal tunnel from overuse of the dominant hand/forearm in computer work. If you use different muscle groups and hold your body in an unnatural position in the performance of your job or recreational activities, those muscles can be subjected to injury/strain. It's important to be mindful of how you hold your body, aka body mechanics, in all your activities. I understand this is difficult to do especially if you're caught up in the busyness of your day, but you must make the conscious decision to be aware and act on it.

After your review of your physical health, is there anything you want to change? Add? Delete? Keep track of these on a separate piece of paper for use in *Step 11 – Establish Your Intentions*.

Mind Health

Let's move on to your mind health. I'm living proof you are what you think. I believed I was a failure after living in San Diego for a year. I believed I was unsuited for an administrative line of work. I believed I was unlovable. I believed I was incapable of raising my grandkids. There was extreme darkness in my mind. I was living to the expectations of outside influences. Instead, I should have been living to the expectations of my inner self, my inner child/my authentic self. However, that part of me was unreachable when I returned to Washington. After five years of reaching and sliding backward in my journey to find my authentic self, I discovered these steps to aid me on my path.

Positive affirmations are my favorite *go-to's*. Are you participating in positive affirmations throughout your day? Are you inundated with negativity, sometimes without even knowing it? Or is society giving you examples of how you should look, how you should act that you can never attain? Are you maintaining an objective outlook to understand these are not realistic? You may feel shamed or envious. How do you release it?

Beginning your day with the four statement mantra of Ho'oponopono is one way (see *Step 4 - Ho'oponopono*): I'm sorry. Please forgive me. Thank you. I love you. Remember, you're saying this to yourself. You own the feelings these pictures generate. You take responsibility for the feelings you have. You take away those feelings of shame and guilt for not meeting this expectation. You get rid of it.

Another way is meditation to ease your way out of this negativity. Similar wording as the Ho'oponopono mantra, you say what makes you feel better. "Creator please instill in me the determination to eat healthy, exercise to my fullest, and adjust my mindset to understand what is attainable for me." Or write your own. (See *Step 9 - Meditate/Reflect on Your Path.*)

Are you keeping self-limiting beliefs out of your mind? We discussed this in *Step 5 - Establish your Beliefs.* You are in control of the positivity of your life. Your glass is full. You are complete.

Are you reading, listening to uplifting content? Are you filling your life with joy? You need to take ownership of this.

I know what it is like to live with negative thoughts. I sabotaged myself with self-limiting beliefs. I grew up in an era where blond, blue-eyed, skinny Barbie dolls were the only dolls around. In my case, and in the case of other girls of my Baby Boomer era, we used our dolls to *play grown-up* with social roles, i.e. mother, housewife, cook. Why wouldn't we assume we had to look like her, too?

One of my goals as a young girl was to have a more common name, Dorothy was the name of choice (thank you Wizard of Oz[6]), to be blond and blue-eyed, and skinny. I vividly remember one Christmas when I was six or so Daelene received a set of plastic wigs as a present. I wanted the wigs badly, and yes, one of them was a blond, bubble hairdo. My gift was a doll as tall as me; it was an amazing and thoughtful present, but I wanted to be that blond-haired girl even if it meant wearing a plastic wig. My worldview was colored by society's expectations; I didn't see or understand the uniqueness my family possessed and that I was part of.

As I grew older, junior high and high school, I still wanted a more common name, lighter eyes, and I still wanted to be skinny. I accepted my hair coloring because I could see the red highlights from my German heritage. None of these wishes came to fruition. One wonders, how this *lack of* influenced my decision making as I was growing up.

This is only one influencer from my life. I could analyze my life and come up with many more. The point is we all have them, these self-limiting beliefs. We need to face them as best we can, sometimes with the help of a therapist/counselor, own them, and change our world view. We need to be ourselves, and we need to remind ourselves daily until this belief that *we are enough* is innate in all we do. I have almost 50 years of programming to change; I will have missteps, but I will continue to persevere. Are you game?

After your review, is there anything you want to change? Add? Delete? Keep track of these on a separate piece of paper for use, in *Step 11 - Establish Your Intentions.*

Spirit Health

Let's move onto spiritual, religious, or *belief in something bigger than us* health. What are your beliefs? Are they uplifting you? Do you have a support structure in this area?

My mother had a negative experience with a church in the mid 1970's. The congregation forced the resignation of the pastor because he or his wife filed for divorce. This contradicted the tenants of church and moved her to stay away from organized religion.

My mother's experience coupled with my own developed the conviction I could nourish my spiritual belief system on my own. However, humans are not meant to be solitary animals. We need to have a family or a tribe around us to support us in like-minded thinking/beliefs. I found if we don't have this support, we tend to backslide into old self-limiting belief habits and forget our purpose and our newfound habits. Society keeps raising its head reminding us we have many things to take care of family, home, work, and the like.

My spiritual support structure is my church. Within its walls, I find a community of like-minded people, yet we all have additional beliefs. All are welcome here in whatever belief system we hold.

Do you have a support structure in place?

After your review, is there anything you want to change? Add? Delete? Keep track of these on a separate piece of paper for use, in *Step 11 - Establish Your Intentions*.

The ultimate goal is to have a positively balanced approach to maintaining your health for your body, mind, and spirit, and to have a self-care routine established. Once you achieve this, you'll be able to give more of yourself to your responsibilities including your purpose. While you want to give of yourself fully, you also need to replenish yourself. If you don't, it will start affecting you with illness, discontent, and unhappiness. As you own these emotions and events, you have the power to change them.

Remember good mind, body and spirit health are your lifestyle choices as well as what you've inherited from your parents/ancestors. Create your own foundation of good habits to pursue and achieve your purpose.

CHAPTER 11

SHAPE YOUR ENVIRONMENT

This chapter outlines three steps to create your inner world.

Step 9 - Meditate for Clarity

What is meditation?

To meditate is to release the busy thoughts of your life by focusing on your breathing or a method of your own choosing and relaxing. You can do this in silence, or by listening to soothing sounds of a drumbeat (shamanic drumming), chanting, ocean waves or other natural sounds. You can meditate for religious/spiritual reasons or as a method of relaxation.

There are as many different reasons to meditate as there are different ways to meditate. Overall, I recommend daily meditation should be added to your self-care routine.

Health Benefits of Meditation: There have been many studies on the health benefits of meditation. The National Center for Complementary and Integrative Health states, "Some research suggests that meditation may physically change the brain and body and could potentially help to improve many health problems and promote healthy behaviors.

- In a 2012 study, researchers compared brain images from 50 adults who meditate and 50 adults who don't meditate. Results suggested that people who practiced meditation for many years have more folds in the outer layer of the brain. This process called gyrification may increase the brain's ability to process information.
- A 2013 review of three studies suggests that meditation may slow, stall, or even reverse changes that take place in the brain due to normal aging.
- Results from a 2012 NCCIH-funded study suggest that meditation can affect activity in the amygdala (a part of the brain involved in processing emotions) and that different types of meditation can affect the amygdala differently even when the person is not meditating.
- Research about meditation's ability to reduce pain has produced mixed results. However, in some studies, scientists suggest that meditation activates certain areas of the brain in response to pain."[7] I count myself one of the *mixed results*. I was in labor with my daughter and I meditated so completely I almost stopped my contractions.

I recommend using meditation for stress relief, to bring inner peace, and as a tool to help manifest what you want in your life (See *Step 11 - Establish Your*

Intentions to help you understand manifestation.). What is this tool using? Energy and the Law of Attraction, as I believe in it.

The Law of Attraction is simply what you focus on you will bring into your life. Some of the things we focus on are what we believe, what we visualize, what words we use, what you talk about, or what you feel strongly about will appear in your life. They are positive, negative, or are neutral.

What we think about will turn into beliefs. Whether we're aware of it or not, we act upon them as described in *Step 5 - Establish Your Beliefs*. So why would you continue to limit yourself when you can empower yourself? Focus on the positive and what you want to happen.

When negative events happen in your life, look for the blessing in the event. Consider them life lessons. What have we learned from them? Turn it into a positive event.

A few of the different ways to meditate are yoga, mindfulness meditation, guided meditation, mantra meditation, and others. I recommend guided meditation, mantra meditation (see *Step 4 - Ho'oponopono* and the four statements), mindfulness meditation (used in *Step 12 - Be Present*). Even listening to raindrops, forest sounds, or the gentle lap of the ocean waves is meditation.

Meditation can be as simple as focusing on one deep breath into your stomach and then filling your chest to the count of four and exhale from your stomach then chest to a count of eight. Or it could encompass a 45 minute or longer session. You can find meditations through an app for your cell phone, on YouTube, in books, and online.

Locations for meditation can be anywhere you have minimal distractions; i.e. at the ocean, in a forest, in front of an altar, (an altar is simply a collection of items that have meaning to you.), in your house, or at work (for the one breath meditation or if you're on a break).

Choose loose-fitting clothing if you're intending to do a longer meditation. Otherwise, wear what you find comfortable.

Position is your choice; however, I don't recommend lying down because you will fall asleep.

Now, close your eyes, breath slowly and deeply, quiet your mind and let the experience of meditation take you on your own special journey.

Step 10 - Positive Self-Talk

Positive Self Talk works well if you say it out loud. Otherwise, you're only thinking about it, and it's not as effective. Open yourself to Creator and pray for divine guidance before you begin.

What is Positive Self-Talk? It can encompass a selection of topics; you can complement yourself in any area of your life, it can be motivational, affirmations, it can be goal/intention setting, or problem-solving. From this point, I'll use *intention setting* for clarity, but it includes goal setting as well.

I use Positive Self-Talk for intention setting, problem-solving, and venting. I take it one step further by recording it to reprocess it when I have time to solely focus on it. That can be accomplished with any recorder app you have on your cell phone. I use Recorder Plus on my iPhone.

The focus in intention setting or problem-solving is to talk as objectively as you can to become your best. Make sure you turn off your self-limiting beliefs, if any are lingering before you begin.

When problem-solving, use your recording device of choice to Self-Talk the situation, the pros and cons, and possible solution. Listen to it later and identify your concerns. Develop an action plan with a reasonable completion date to change your situation into a positive one.

When intention setting use the same steps as above. Remember to work your intentions as you would your vision board. Lastly, evaluate your steps to see if they're viable.

Everyone knows what venting is. Instead of sharing it with someone pour your frustration with no filter onto the recorder. If you share it with a person instead of the recorder, what you say may hit a chord with them. They want to stay objective for you, but they may become biased to the topic of your frustration. This may add another layer of issues you have to deal with.

I vent to my recorder and delete it if no workable information is on it. The act of venting is solution enough for me, most of the time, to approach the situation objectively. If I need more time to process, I'll continue to vent, and the answers become clear.

Another step I use is to transcribe the recording to a word-processing program. The transcription helps me analyze my solution further to ensure I am utilizing my empowering beliefs and disregarding any lingering self-limiting beliefs.

Positive Self-Talk should be kept on your Intentional Living toolbelt. Even if you have a trusted friend or loved one to vent to, Positive Self-Talk is a tool you should utilize. You express your frustration, recognize it for being a trigger, stop it from reverting to a self-limiting belief, and turn it into an empowering one.

Step 11 - Establish Your Intentions

Why should we establish our intentions? I believe if we don't know the path we should be on, we'll be meandering down roads which will lead us away from our purpose. While I agree some spontaneity is desirable, we can achieve it when we're headed in the right direction.

I think everyone wants to feel they've made an impact in their life. It's defining this *impact* which differentiates us. Again, I know I'm stating the obvious to some, but we are all at different points in our lives, thus our definition of impact is unique to each one of us.

My worldview as a young child was colored by trauma. I continued to make choices based on this skewed worldview for the following four decades. The trauma was a silent partner in all my relationships, and I wasn't aware of it.

I didn't know who I truly was without acknowledging how the trauma affected me. My authentic self was hidden for decades. I couldn't truly know my purpose without knowing me. The goals I set at my younger ages weren't constructed with the full knowledge I needed.

I am a 59-year-old example of *it's never too late* to do anything worth doing. Finding your authentic self, your purpose, and your path is worth doing. Sticking to your path, with guidance from Creator, is also worth doing.

We stick to our path through intentional living.

There are different reasons to set intentions as there are different time frames.

For example, when I walk into a massage room, I set an intention for a specific outcome for the patient. From an analytical point of view and the massage referral from the doctor or chiropractor, you identify body areas to treat which will provide the biggest impact for pain relief, increased mobility, and increased range of motion. This translates into an increased ability to do the activities of daily living all in concert with the ability of your patient. Further intention is set with the number of treatments the patient will need with a re-evaluation scheduled at the end to determine the need for further treatment.

My intention for the massage session is not only analytical but includes energy healing, too. I purposefully pray for the patient to connect to Creator, their angels, and their guides so the Divine beings aid in the patient's healing. I ask Creator to guide my hands for the patient's best and highest good.

Setting both intentions of asking for Divine healing as well as engaging my skill as a therapist establishes the partnership between me and the patient for their path to recovery.

When and how do you set your intentions? Do you set them for your work? Setting an intention and an affirmation can be the same words such as "I am having a productive day. I am studying effectively for the test tomorrow." And it could be as in my example above.

Setting an intention can be to act on something, but the byproduct of that action hurts another person. Your intention is not to hurt the person, but the crafting of your action, which you choose not to change as the outcome is important, does cause hurt anyway. When the time is right, and you will know, you should reach out to the person and apologize for the effects of your action.

My intention to move to San Diego was important. My removal of Jasper and Juliet from Washington hurt my ex-husband, the children's grandad, Joe. It was not my intention to hurt Joe.

What does setting intentions for a specific period look like?

If you're strong in knowing who you are and what your life path should look like, then it's simply a matter of recording your intent and following through on it.

What does this mean? Let me share an old New Year's story. The word *resolution* has never set well with me. I hear in my head I resolve to do this, that, or the other. It has a negative connotation for me which means what I choose to resolve had been a problem previously.

This is not how I want to envision the new year ahead. I want to set intentions of events, milestones, daily choices. They are my purpose, not a problem to solve.

Instead, I'd set intentions. I write them down in a positive affirmational way. *I am eating nutritional food. I exercise every day. I meditate every morning.* To give it more importance I'd light a white candle and recite my intentions. Afterwards, I put the paper in a notebook I intend to look at every day. I read the notebook every day for a week, then I'd miss a day. I read them on consecutive days for another four days. February rolls around, life set in with all the various responsibilities, and my intentions are buried. They aren't written in words I can easily recall so they don't come up as an *oh, I remember now.* Then it's time to set new intentions for the new year.

If we're fortunate, we'll remember our intentions. If we do remember, most of us will leave it as set on a pre-established course and forget to re-check to ensure we're still on the same path. How often do we go with the flow of life, and now are on an unexpected, but not an unwelcome path, and are at a loss to figure out how we got there?

Rechecking your intentions periodically is crucial to the success of intention setting. Also, forgiveness of self is important when you don't meet the intentions you set.

We are focusing with great determination on what we choose to bring into our lives. Again, what we focus on, whether positive or negative, we will manifest. It is important to focus on the positive aspects you want to manifest in your life. Banish the worry, the self-limiting beliefs, and other negativity.

I've shared that my mother's death was the catalyst for my journey into self. I initiated changes in my life, found my purpose, and set intentions. These intentions were more profound, and I took action on them.

However, they weren't well thought out, nor was there a subsequent series of intentions established as the second step in the manifestation process. I achieved my intentions of moving to San Diego and getting the children settled but didn't set intentions past that. Intentions for employment and for the children's life after moving should have been set. I could have avoided a lot of the heartache if I had rechecked my path.

Much knowledge was gained from my journey to San Diego. I learned I'm a strong manifestor. I also learned setting intentions and manifesting is like a section of a book. You're not finished when you've reached the end of the section. The book continues and you must also.

I was lost but I shouldn't have worried. Creator was there for me.

Creator is always putting messages in front of us, and we need to pay attention. Creator provided me a snippet of information about vision boards. I researched it and the proverbial light bulb went on. This was the tool I needed to set my intentions and keep track of them.

It is part of my purpose to share this tool with you.

Are you ready to set your intentions for your life, or for a job at hand? Let's get started!

First a little background. For those who don't know, a vision board is a tool to display what you want to manifest (bring) into your life using the Law of Attraction. Did you know Oprah Winfrey, Jack Canfield, John Assaraf, and others use a vision board to manifest what they wish in their lives? You can, too.

Some of you may be thinking, "Well of course, these famous people can manifest things in their lives. They have the money and prestige to do it." However, they were creating vision boards before they were household names and bringing in seven-figure incomes.

The Law of Attraction (LoA) is the Creator bringing to you what you focus on. The Creator doesn't differentiate between positive or negative; it brings you what you think about. So be positive, always, as like attracts like.

Let's dive into how to create a vision board.

Vision Board:

I. PLAN

a. The first step is to determine what you want to manifest in your life. Do you want positive changes in your health, career, physical needs, your values, family life, love life, what you want to learn, and/or how you spend your free time, etc.? You can select many or only one area to focus on.

b. Next, you should outline in detail what you want to manifest. The Universe will provide you what you ask for. Sometimes you don't know the details of what you want so you list it in as specific terms as you know.

c. Select a time frame for completion for your intentions.

Planning takes a bit of time so it's important that you allow yourself all the time you need.

II. PREP

If you're creating an annual Vision Board, you'll want to collect magazines in the areas you think you'll be setting your intentions around October for a November/ December assembly. It's sometimes difficult to find the picture in a magazine that best illustrates your intention, but there's always the internet.

You'll need the following supplies:

- ☐ Magazines
- ☐ Scissors
- ☐ Glue
- ☐ Thick poster board
- ☐ Pictures from the internet, and/or words or phrases that have meaning to you.

III. PREPARE

How you mount your pictures/words/phrases is entirely up to you.

I find best practice is to place your focus in the center column of your Vision Board. The intentions with the highest priority are placed in the center. Other intentions are placed as you feel called to mount them.

a. I believe a Clutter-Free Vision Board is best as I want the Universe to see with clarity what I am manifesting in my life.

b. In the Messy Vision Board, the items are placed on top of each other. I don't advocate this method as I'll explain in the Be Present section.

Ultimately, the design is your decision.

After your vision board has been completed, you need to work it. See below on how to work it.

IV. BE PRESENT

Now what? Your Vision Board is complete. What do you do with it?

Best practice is to hang it in a place you'll see it twice a day.

Now it's time to work your Vision Board. What does this mean? Best practice includes the four following steps. As you become more adept at manifestation, you'll add, delete, or replace steps to make it your own process.

a. Visualization/Meditation Exercises.

Your Vision Board is strategically placed. This is where a Clutter-Free Vision Board is important. You need to be able to narrow your focus quickly and efficiently, and you want the Universe to do the same. A Messy Vision Board causes confusion, and lack of focus. Clarity attracts, confusion repels.

Look at it, close your eyes, and visualize owning the intention for two minutes twice daily. If the Intention is very important, you can engage in 10 to 15 minute meditations visualizing the above in more detail, using self-talk affirmations, and welcome Divine guidance.

b. Pro-Active Steps.

Visualization with or without meditation will not produce results alone. The Creator hears what you're asking for, and your brain is processing your thinking into a belief system. Self-limiting thoughts and behaviors are minimized to be replaced with positive thought and action. The Universe is lining up opportunities. Your mission is to be receptive and act.

Now, your mindset is on how to complete your Intention. What steps do you need to accomplish it? Best practice is to accomplish at least one or two things a day towards accomplishing your Intention.

c. Re-Check of Intentions.

Your Vision Board is your personal business plan with yourself and the Creator. It is best practice to review your Vision Board periodically.

If it's an annual or project-based Vision Board, I recommend a monthly review. As you've worked your intentions, you'll have achieved clarity, thus your Vision Board blueprint will need revision. This can be as simple as adding or crossing off action steps.

I recommend a quarterly evaluation and possible re-write of your Intentions if your clarity has added details which need to be accounted for. I had to do this for my Writing Intention. You need to have as many details for your Intention as possible so you're able to visualize yourself achieving it.

d. Be Open to the Creator.

Finally, be open to the messages from the Creator. They can be subtle, or in your face, or anywhere in between. The Creator provides these opportunities for your best and highest good. They could offer forward progress on your path, or they could be life lessons you need to learn. In either case, they're needed for your continued growth.

Does this sound complicated or over the top to you? Is this too much effort to complete? Since completing the first draft of this book Daelene shared with me another celebrity has announced his use of vision boards, Steve Harvey, and his challenge to everyone in the studio audience to start using one, too. Here is the link to his video https://youtu.be/_LBJdqTYj24.

Why do I keep sharing about celebrities? Because they're the ones you'll notice. If I said Jane Doe used a vision board to manifest her house, would you be interested?

What if I told you I manifested my house, significant monetary abundance, spiritual growth, and my book journey from my 2018 vision board? This is why the steps I've shared with you are so detailed.

I created my vision board on December 31st, 2017. I used the clutter-free style because I wanted Creator to see what I wanted to manifest in 2018. This style is easier for me to meditate on. In the center of my board I put the important things; my house, my writing journey, and monetary abundance. On the sides were other things I wanted in my life, but I didn't focus on them as deliberately as I did the middle.

Interestingly, while I was focusing on the three in the middle, the other things were manifesting as well. My spiritual growth, nutrition information and source of meal planning (which I ignored as I was comfort eating while I was processing the trauma I experienced), exercise and perseverance all came to fruition without my direct focus to various levels.

My house intention was placed on my vision board on December 31st, 2017. I purchased my house on January 19th and moved in on March 5th. I did extra Law of Attraction meditating which included visualizing me holding the key to my house in my hand and unlocking my door.

I received a significant monetary abundance in October, but I have been receiving varying amounts throughout the year.

My book journey has been the most profound. Creator put the steps in front of me and I followed. I've been dreaming of writing and publishing a book since I was 22. That's a total 36 years on and off. Then Creator led me to Author Academy Elite (AAE) in July 2018. This book will be published in Summer 2019.

Do I need to continue to promote vision boards?

CHAPTER 12

EMBODY YOUR CHANGE

This chapter presents two steps to implement habits to maintain your authentic self.

Step 12 - Be Present

To be present means you are focused on the now, this very moment, and aware of all that is important in the task at hand. You are grounded and not thinking of the future. It's easy to be knocked off stride if this is not your norm.

I woke up this morning full of optimism, light-hearted, ready to greet the world. I sat down to write this afternoon and all motivation had left me.

What changed?

Outside events I didn't have control over happened and I allowed them to derail me.

Three events, back to back, hit me hard and knocked me off my stride for four hours. Honestly, one of the three tore my heart a bit, which made it easier for the rest to affect me negatively.

This is when the proverbial light bulb went on, and I realized I was allowing these events to derail me. I used Positive Self-Talk to get back on track. I wrote an email to myself trying to problem solve my immobilization. It took the edge off the pain, but I was still slogging through my responsibilities.

We need to remember the people closest to us are the ones who can inflict the harshest pain. We're not always ready to deflect the pain so it's important to practice the tools I'm sharing until they become a habit. Living your authentic life and overcoming this conditioning is challenging, especially at the beginning of your journey.

The pain in my heart isn't gone, but it's eased enough so I can function.

To 'Be Present' is to be aware of and focused on the details of the intentions you set in *Step 11 - Establish Your Intentions.*

Don't get caught up in ordinary life where you fail to see your purpose.

Step 13 - Anticipate, Recognize, and Address Your Setbacks

You've done it! You've freed your authentic self or are a work in progress. Your purpose is in sight. Your tribe is supporting you and your family and close friends may be among them. You're making progress on your path, and life is great. You've been meditating daily or utilizing another tool to maintain focus and strength in knowing who you are. You are systematically dismissing your self-limiting beliefs and lifting up your empowering beliefs to stay positive.

You notice things are not quite as smooth in your family. The changes you've made may be making some of them uncomfortable.

This is anticipating possible setbacks.

You know communication is key to calming their fears; talk with them to resolve this issue so it doesn't derail you.

You've anticipated, recognized, and addressed a possible setback.

What happens if you're blind-sided by family who doesn't want to change, move forward, and want you to go back? You don't anticipate the train wreck now sitting inside of your heart space. You can't focus. You're untethered from your path. How do you recover?

If you've established the practice of meditation, you'll easily start the process of recovery when you ready yourself for your daily meditation ritual. You'll fall into the rote movement and exercise of readying yourself to delve into yourself. Allow your unconscious mind to take over and walk you back onto your path.

If you've not had the chance to establish a routine to sustain your authenticity, use the Ho'oponopono mantra to bring you back to center.

This doesn't mean it'll all come together again. It might not, but you'll be able to pick up the pieces and gather them to your heart space to regain the presence of mind once again.

Utilizing some of the tools learned here, Positive Self-Talk whether it is utilized with a recorder or having a conversation with yourself, is invaluable to getting back to your purpose.

What if ordinary life slips unnoticed into your path? Life becomes too busy for you to take that first right step. Are you boxed in your thinking? Have you reverted to self-limiting beliefs without realizing it? This happened to me for over four years. It's easy to do. Staying strong in your authentic self is foreign. You're accustomed to doing for others and not yourself.

Stop making excuses why you can't take those action steps you identified. You're the only one who can make the changes. You have to want the changes. Nothing will help you unless you're ready to make that first right step.

Walk in your authenticity. Minimize the time you've reverted to self-limiting beliefs, to finally standing tall in who you are and your purpose.

"To the world, you may be one person;
but to one person you may be the world."
— Dr. Seuss

That one person needs your insight; remember your message is bigger than your fears.

AFTERWORD

There are a few unanswered questions to how things turned out upon moving back to Washington.

Mom's ashes are contained in a wind chime hung on my front porch. She sings when the wind blows, and sometimes when the air is still. I know my mom is always with me, and I feel her love every day.

I was angry with my brother, Michael, for a very long time. His rejection cut me to the heart. It has taken me decades to forgive, and ultimately understand it was the chemicals and his belief he *wasn't enough* that caused him to leave my letters unopened. He hadn't felt worthy. I wish he was here today so I could tell him it never mattered about his drug use. I would tell him, "I see you. I have always loved you for who you are."

Jasper and Juliet wanted a house to live in and it made sense. They were too young to be home alone, so we rented a house near Joe, Jr. and Emma. The kids rode the bus to their house after school. I missed them while I was at work, but I never worried or felt guilty because they were with family.

Joe, Jr., Emma, and the kids came to visit us in San Diego. He forgave me for leaving. However, melding with family when we returned to Washington was a little difficult. Life hadn't stopped while we were gone, and they had developed different dynamics which we didn't fit into. Everyone was uncomfortable at first, but we persevered, and our relationships are strong, yet different.

Victoria has found her feet and is making a home for herself and Rachel. She also has a strong bond with Jasper and Juliet.

Daelene and I made up, too, while I lived in San Diego. Our connection became stronger because of our disagreement.

Strong, yet different describes Mike and my relationship. We didn't know if we would continue after the kids and I moved back. After several months we started talking again, but it was tense. One day we hashed it all out, and we eased back into a semblance of the way we were before the move to San Diego.

As with everything we encountered there were small nuances which shifted. This applied to Mike and me, also. Our outlook had matured and we both recognized the children fared better with family they grew up with.

The kids had support in Washington—they could see their little sisters, their mom, their uncle, auntie, and cousins, occasionally their father, their granddad, and their great-aunties. They settled into the same schools as their cousins, Anthony and Marie. This was important for them. Mike appreciated the need for stability for the children and for me.

Mike and I are living in the now. We have a loose outline of our future relationship. When the kids finish high school, we'll figure out how we go from there. For right now, we are the epitome of a long-distance relationship. We are loving, committed to each other, and try to fill up our lives with ordinary moments-sharing our day with each other as if we were in the same town. We see each other four to six times a year, always with a ten-day visit during the summer. Jasper and Juliet share in the ten-day visit every other year.

Joe and I are friends and are connected by our love for Jasper and Juliet. We work hard to do what's best for them.

I love my massage therapy career. To be part of a patient's healing process is humbling and important to me. I will eventually age out of some techniques, but not in the near future. The modalities which require less strenuous movement will enhance the treatments I offer. They are focused energy work, Reiki, Lymphatic Drainage, and TMJ treatment for now. I'll be gaining new skills each year to include other healing arts.

INTENTIONAL LIVING

When I began this book journey I didn't know exactly where we would travel to, and I am glad you joined me. I hope you have found the overall message of the book has resonated with you because we are the same in many aspects.

Trauma, struggles, and self-limiting beliefs strike at the core of who we are, and we can overcome them together to establish our empowering beliefs, find our authentic selves, and fulfill our purpose. Here we are the same, and I encourage you to become a Phoenix Rising with me.

We've come to the end of the book, but not the end of our journey. For we are ever evolving to become more knowledgeable, more confident, and more skilled in our empowering beliefs.

We are building up the levels of positivity and higher vibrations to be closer to Creator and our purpose. The more open we become, the more opportunities we will see and act on.

This is the beginning of our Intentional Living.

APPENDIX 1

DISCUSSION POINTS*

Chapter 1, Remember Your Past is to remind us not only traditions are handed down, but also trauma, cultural beliefs, and world events that affected our parents, and their extended families are inherited.

1. Do you have anger at your parents'? What are you angry about?

2. Think it through. What did your parents experience as they were growing up? How did their experiences shape their lives? Did it affect their parenting styles, their beliefs?

3. Is any of their behavior while you were growing up forgivable? Forgive as you're the only one who drags this burden with you. Forgiveness frees you to move forward and not be stuck in the past.

Chapter 2, Replicate Their Environment speaks to how our parents' life experiences, whether negative or positive, impact their world view and how they choose to live. While their intentions are to raise us the best way they can, sometimes their beliefs and behaviors are ingrained and cannot help but affect their parenting. Thus, they have replicated their environment and the blank canvas all babies are purported to be born with is already painted on.

1. Were you surrounded by fear-based-decision-making when you were a child?
2. Were you expected to keep secrets and didn't know why? Were you expected to keep secrets or else?
3. Did you experience trauma as a young child?

Chapter 3, Clean Your Canvas is to remind us we can wipe off all that has been written on our canvas, and repaint our path.

1. Did your parent's beliefs/world view become a layer over your identity?
2. Did you have dreams and aspirations of your own, or were they projected upon you?
3. Were you able to stand your ground, and follow your dreams?

Chapter 4, Accepting Their Identity is written to illustrate how pervasive our environment and nurturing is in the development of our values and identity. Is this truly who we are? If some feel right, then keep them. If they don't resonate, delete them.

1. After you reached your majority what framework were you living with?

2. Was it your parent's/environmental framework, or one of your own design?

3. Upon reflection, how do you feel about this?

Chapter 5, Reframe Your Reflection is a reminder we have the power to live our purpose. We don't have to become what circumstance forces us to be nor live according to how society/family defines us. I recognize this is easy to say and takes a lot of courage to embrace and walk your change.

1. Are you living in cognizance with your true self and purpose?

2. Are there facets of you which are not of your choosing?

3. At the end of your life, will you have regrets?

Chapter 6, Face Your Reality is truly seeing yourself in the mirror for who you are, making your first right step, how this will affect the people in your life, and their reaction to your forward progress.

1. Have you tried to live your truths and were met with negativity?

2. Did your self-limiting beliefs overpower you?

3. Did you fold under the pressure or did you persevere and continue?

4. What is trying to "bubble up" for you?

In *Chapter 7, Live Their Existence*, the adages, *hindsight is 20/20, practice makes perfect, and look before you leap,* define what should have been done at this point in my life.

One is in a state of euphoria after reaching your epiphany—finding your purpose and identity; essentially your blinders have been taken off and you're aching to start living your authenticity. Remember, mindfulness in all you do is key. *Think critically, plan carefully, and move deliberately with trusted and like-minded advisors.*

We are birthing our identity and purpose; it is not a clear path. We have years of conditioning to expel from our psyche while we are living in our truth. We will revert to previous self-limiting beliefs when faced with stressors if we haven't lived (practiced) our truth for a long period of time. So, it's essential to move mindfully as you're stepping onto your true path before taking that huge leap into what you think you know.

1. Have you tried something new and did it backfire on you?

2. If it did backfire, what choice did you make?

3. What will you do now?

The despair in *Chapter 8, End My Life*, only happened because I allowed myself to believe I was the sum total of my self-limiting beliefs. I believed I was worthless, lacked value, unwanted, and unlovable. I lost sight of my true identity and essence.

These were all lies. Did I have all the answers? Absolutely not, but Creator did. I was course corrected back on my path.

1. Do you sense something is missing from your life?

2. Can you identify it?

3. Have you tried a new plan for your life?

4. Were you successful, and how did you react?

5. Were you unsuccessful, and how did you react?

Chapter 9, Restrict Your Progress, speaks to how you are your own worst enemy without realizing it, even after you've experienced your epiphany. It is easy to fall back into old habits of self-limiting beliefs and following societal dictates. It takes a slap to the back of the head to course correct us to our true passion, our true path.

Welcome to the adventure of living your authenticity from visualization to actualization, of overcoming the imposter inside, discovering who you truly are, and implementing habits to maintain your authentic self.

1. Have you ever thought about what your purpose is?

2. Have you allowed 'life' to get in the way of your purpose?

3. Do you want to find your identity or purpose?

*There are so many ways to process information depending on how comfortable you are with the material. Some can discuss the topics with others, and others will journal. I found the process of Positive Self-Talk met my needs the best only if I recorded it, processed it while listening, and finally transcribed it.

Use your recording device of choice to Positive Self-Talk the situation, the pros and cons, and possible solution. Listen to it later and identify your concerns. Develop an action plan to change your situation into a positive one. Transcribe it if you need further clarification.

APPENDIX 2

NOTES

CHAPTER 8: END MY LIFE?

1 **National Suicide Prevention Lifeline**
https://suicidepreventionlifeline.org
1-800-273-8255

CHAPTER 9: RESTRICT YOUR PROGRESS

2 University of Pittsburgh Medical Center (UPMC), Neurosurgery, The Science Behind Procrastination, July 28, 2015
https://share.upmc.com/2015/07/the-science-behind-procrastination/

STEP 8: MAINTAIN YOUR HEALTH

3 Bryant Stamford, Professor and Chairman, Department of Kinesiology and Integrative Physiology, Hanover College, 2014
https://www.courier-journal.com/story/life/wellness/2014/04/03/use-muscles-lose/7257291/

[4] U.S. Department of Health & Human Service, National Heart, Blood, Lung Institute
https://www.nhlbi.nih.gov/health-topics/sleep-deprivation-and-deficiency

[5] MAYO Clinic, Healthy Lifestyle, Nutrition and Healthy Eating, September 6, 2017 https://www.mayoclinic.org/healthy-lifestyle/nutrition-and-healthy-eating/in-depth/water/art-20044256

[6] *The Wizard of Oz*. Directed by Victor Fleming. By Noel Langley, Florence Ryerson, Edgar Alan Woolf, Herbert Stothart, E. Y. Harburg, Harold Arlen, Georgie Stoll, George Bassman, Murray Cutter, Bobby Connolly, Harold Rosson, Douglas Shearer, Arnold Gillespie, and Blanche Sewell. Produced by Mervyn LeRoy, Cedric Gibbons, William A. Horning, Edwin B. Willis, Adrian, and Jack Dawn. Performed by Judy Garland, Frank Morgan, Ray Bolger, Bert Lahr, Jack Haley, Billie Burke, Margaret Hamilton, Charles Grapewin, and Clara Blandick. United States: Metro Goldwyn Mayer Presents, 1939. Television.

STEP 9: MEDITATE FOR CLARITY

[7] National Center for Complimentary and Integrative Health, US Department of Health and Human Services, issued *Meditation: In Depth*, Meditation and the Brain, NCCIH Pub No.: D308, Last Updated: April 2016.
https://nccih.nih.gov/health/meditation/overview.htm#hed1

ACKNOWLEDGEMENTS

Writing this book was harder than I thought, and without the support of many people it wouldn't have come to fruition. Heartfelt thanks go to my best friends, my sisters, Daelene and Donnette. We agonized over the traumas, laughed at the quirkiness of dad and mom, and loved on each other. Your love, encouragement, and support are the wind beneath my wings.

To Mike without your love, understanding, and support as I agonized over the telling of my story, without your objective observations over the last year, and without you standing with me in my truth I would have been hard pressed to create what I have. You are my rock.

To my family. To my son 'Joe, Jr. and his wife who is a daughter to me, 'Emma', your continued support and love when life became tough, and even when it wasn't, is embedded in my heart forever. To my daughter, 'Victoria', whose touches in my life helped ease over some of the rough times as I wrote this book. To all my grandchildren, 'Anthony', 'Jasper', 'Juliet', 'Marie', 'Nicole', and 'Rachel' you inspire me to be the best I can be. To 'Karen'—thank you for being there for me at a very low point in my life. To Nani, my sister from another mister, thank you for always telling me of the light you see in me.

To Kary Oberbrunner, CEO of Author Academy Elite and so much more, thank you for following your passion. If you hadn't, I wouldn't be where I am today. You and your team are the epitome of service with coaching, supporting, and providing a plethora of resources to help us be Souls on Fire.

To my editors, Nansi and Nanette, thank you for your keen insight and editorial help in birthing my book baby. To my Beta readers: with your invaluable help the raw book you read has matured into what you hold in your hands today. Thank you, Ann, Jackie, Daelene, Mike, Michele, and Sarah.

Finally to all those who have been part of my getting here: Cristie, Florci, Lisa, Elisa, Stephanie, Janene, Melissa, Ginger, Sam, Diana, Evelyn, Sarah, Alma, Rosie, Betty, Marla, Courtney, Corinn, and Chelsey—thank you.

Without all of you in my life, I wouldn't have had the strength to write this book. Your support was in the little touches and in the big ones when I let loose of my grief and pain. You are all human angels, and I am blessed.

ABOUT THE AUTHOR

DARCEY KESNER HAWKINS is a Phoenix Rising. Through her writing , speaking, mentoring, and healing arts she helps people overcome the imposter inside, discover who they truly are, and implement habits to maintain their authentic self.

Darcey is one of the masses who has struggled with finding out Who Is That in the Mirror?, what her passion is, and how to serve her community. Darcey's journey began with generational trauma, a sense of not belonging, and insecurity. She never felt "good enough". These self-limiting beliefs followed her into young adult hood where she threw herself into society's expectation of 'normal'. She became wife, mother, employee, full time student, caretaker; always striving to 'become' but never achieving it—until now.

Today, Darcey is a wise elder with years of experience and pain behind her. She invests in people beginning with her two grandchildren she is raising, care taking her mother for several years, and mentoring others in their personal growth. She lives in Washington with her two grandchildren, and two black 'panthers'.

YOUR NEXT STEPS WITH BECOMING

A PHOENIX RISING

THROUGH INTENTIONAL LIVING

DarceyKesnerHawkins.com

CPSIA information can be obtained
at www.ICGtesting.com
Printed in the USA
LVHW041016190819
628119LV00002B/79/P